PARENT'S
GUIDE
TO
WASHINGTON
PUBLIC
SCHOOLS

Parent's Guide to Washington Public Schools

BY TONY BASTIAN

Acknowledgements

THANKS TO THE TEACHERS, principals, school board directors, and *especially parents* who shared their questions and concerns with me. Thanks also to the state employees of Washington, especially those at the Office of the Superintendent of Public Instruction — you were always helpful and knowledgeable. The law library staff at the University of Washington were great guides to finding the right information. And thank you to Scott Miners, Dixie Hughes, Sue Monin, Diane Franchini, Marvin Norman, Ron Swanson, Jessica Vogel, Neil Theobald, Gene and Elma Willey, Vicki Anderson, Marc and Heidi Genty, Julia Wentz, Dawn and Randy Stoner, and Karl Fynboe. I am grateful to my parents and my wife for all their encouragement.

Contents

Part I. Students

Part II. Teachers

Part III. Schools

A Note on the Sources

Material for this book was drawn from a variety of state laws, school documents, interviews, and education organizations. Among those, Washington statute law and case law need some explaining.

Sometimes a footnote reads: RCW 28A.150.020.

The Revised Code of Washington (RCW) is state law, passed by the legislature and signed by the governor. The 28A stands for Title 28A, the state laws that pertain to schools. The remaining numbers signify the chapter and section within Title 28A.

Other times a footnote reads: WAC 180-30-125.

The Washington Administrative Code (WAC) has several titles that pertain to education. Title 180 identifies the source as the rules and regulations of the State Board of Education. Title 392 identifies the rules and regulations of the Superintendent of Public Instruction. The remaining numbers signify the chapter and section within those titles. These administrative laws interpret and give more detail than the Revised Code of Washington.

The Common School Manual contains all these rules and regulations and is the source for almost all law that has bearing on the schools.

This reference guide also uses case law to determine Washington educational policies. The full text of these decisions can be found at any County Courthouse or university law library. The following examples show how to read those references.

A Washington State Court of Appeals case:
State v. Slattery 56 Wn.App 820 (1990)

Washington Appellate Reports, volume 56, page 820, decided in 1990

A Washington Supreme Court case:
Wagenblast v. Odessa School District 110 Wn.2d 845 (1988) Washington Reports Second Series, volume 110, page 845, decided in 1988

A United States Supreme Court Case:
Washington v. Seattle School District 102 S.Ct 3187 (1987) Supreme Court Reporter, volume 102, page 3187, decided in 1987

State court cases originate in one of thirty Superior Courts. From there a case may be appealed to one of the three Courts of Appeals (Seattle, Tacoma, and Spokane) and from there to the Washington Supreme Court in Olympia.

Washington's federal cases start in one of two United States District Courts (Eastern and Western Washington). From there, a case may be appealed to the United States Court of Appeals Ninth District, (based in San Francisco), and from there to the Supreme Court.

Court decisions may only be appealed on a point of law. That is, the appeals court will examine the lower court decision to see if correct legal principles were applied to the facts. The appeals court does not re-examine the facts of the case as previously established by the trial court.

Most legal disputes involving schools are settled in the state courts because education law is usually state, not federal, law. However, when a constitutional issue is at stake, the case will more likely be pursued through the federal courts.

Foreword

THE PURPOSE OF THIS BOOK is to give parents clear answers to commonly asked questions about Washington's public schools. It is based on the simple but accurate notion that school children do better when parents are involved with their education.

For parents to make the best choices for their child's education, they need to understand how the school system works, what their rights as parents are, and what is available to their children. The purpose of this book is to help them.

Parents can use this reference guide in several ways. It is a resource for answering specific questions about Washington's school system. The book is also a starting point for getting more information and greater guidance about a whole range of education topics.

The subjects covered are not comprehensive but then no work on public education ever is. Schools adopt new policies, state laws change, and the courts decide new disputes. However, over the past twenty years, parental rights have steadily grown to allow them the opportunity to shape their child's education more than ever before—that trend is sure to continue.

If this resource guide has a theme, it is that parents have the right and the duty to involve themselves with the schools. It is said that democracy is a participative sport—nowhere should that be more true than in the public schools.

Part I — Students

Attendance

Do children have to go to school?

YES. PARENTS ARE RESPONSIBLE for their child's full-time school attendance from the age of 8 until the child reaches 18. However, they may choose what sort of schooling the child receives. The child may attend a secular private school, or a church school, or be taught at home by a parent. The child may also be excused because of mental or physical handicaps and so attend a residential type of school.

When may a child leave school?

IF A CHILD is at least 15 and has met graduation requirements, or is deemed proficient in the subjects taught in grades 1-9, or is employed in a useful manner at that age, then the child does not necessarily have to attend school.[1]

What if a child fails to attend school?

SCHOOL OFFICIALS TAKE A SERIES OF STEPS to correct a student's un-excused absences from school. First, the school informs the child's parents in writing that a conference is necessary to determine the cause of the absenteeism. The school may adjust the student's classes or provide more individual, possibly remedial, instruction. School officials also encourage and help parents to get outside social services. If the above steps do not succeed, then a school district's attendance officer, or the parents themselves, may petition the juvenile courts to assume jurisdiction over the matter.[2]

May a school official fetch absent students?

YES. TO ENFORCE ATTENDANCE, school districts appoint attendance officers who have the authority to retrieve students ages 8-14 and take them to their parents or to their school. The parents or the student's employer may be fined no more than $25.00/day for this violation. The child is not fined but must start attending school.[3]

Does attendance count in a student's grade?

POSSIBLY. "EACH SCHOOL DISTRICT board of directors may establish student grading policies which permit teachers to consider a student's attendance in determining the student's overall grade or deciding whether the student should be granted or denied credit."[4] However, teachers must also take into account why the student was so often missing from class; there is no penalty for legitimate absences.

Location

What determines where a child attends school?

AS A GENERAL RULE, school districts make an effort to ensure that students attend the school nearest their home. If the nearest school is not possible, than the next nearest school is tried. This situation cannot always be met; the student may require special education, or the way from home to the nearest school may be blocked, or the nearest school may be overcrowded. Under these conditions the local school board might send the child to another school.

Can parents choose another school?

SOMETIMES. Parents may request that their child attend another school in or outside their resident school district. Acceptable reasons for choosing an outside school would be "if the financial, educational, safety, or health conditions affecting the student would likely be reasonably improved as a result of the transfer."[5] Other valid reasons to grant a transfer are for the student to attend a school closer to a parent's work place or to finish-up the last grade at the school where the student had gone before moving. Parents or students denied a transfer may appeal the decision to the Superintendent of Public Instruction.

Does a child have a right to attend any school?

NOT ALWAYS. Parents may have to prove that their child's educational needs simply cannot be met at their local school but can be met elsewhere.

Parents in North River (Pacific County) wanted a release from the local school district so that their two children could attend school in the Cosmopolis (Gray Harbor County) school district. They claimed that the Cosmopolis schools had better instruction because of special remedial reading instructors trained in special education. They also claimed that the North River schools gave conflicting reports on how well their children were doing; grades and assessments were high while test results showed learning problems. The school board turned down the parent's request, as did the Superintendent of Public Instruction who said "the existence of an allegedly superior educational program in another district does not, in and of itself, establish a special hardship."

The case entered the courts and eventually ended with the Washington Supreme Court agreeing with the school district. The majority of justices declined to turn a "disparity among school districts into a constitutional violation of 'basic education.'" Dissenting justices found the majority opinion contradictory: a law that allows students to transfer for "educational improvement" should not be denied because disparities exist between school districts.[6]

What about the new state law on choice?

BEGINNING WITH THE 1992-93 SCHOOL YEAR, parents will have the option to send their child to any *public*, (but not *private* school) in the state. State "basic education" funding will then follow the child to the chosen school rather than going to the student's residential school district. Residential school districts may not refuse to let a child transfer to another school. However, serving school districts can limit non-residential enrollment in each of its schools and so refuse to let "all-comers" enroll at a particularly popular school. The serving district may also choose to charge a fee to transferring students. The fee may be based on the "local levy per student" to offset the extra expenses of the student (as the serving district does not get the local property tax from the student's parents).

Each year, district staff will determine the number of open slots in each school and make this information available to the public. By April 1, districts will choose, *by lottery*, the

5

students accepted for the upcoming year. This random drawing will determine the order of selection for those who applied. Students not selected in the drawing will join an ordered waiting list in case openings become available.[7]

What about busing?

BUSING TO ACHIEVE RACIAL BALANCE in the public schools is a constitutional issue that essentially overrides state laws. The reasoning is that freedom of parental choice in regard to schools cannot be used to re-segregate schools.

Washington's 1978 initiative that prohibited school authorities from transferring students for desegregation reasons did not hold up in court. In 1982, the Supreme Court found that "despite its facial neutrality there was little doubt that the initiative was effectively drawn for racial purposes" and "was carefully tailored to interfere only with desegregation busing."[8] Citing the Fourteenth Amendment, the Court found the law unconstitutional in that it denied equal protection of the law to racial minorities by forbidding mandatory school assignments for almost all reasons except racial ones. Meanwhile, the Seattle school district, among others, had a duty to eliminate segregated schools.

Is the busing matter resolved?

NOT REALLY. The close 5-4 decision and the changing make-up of the Supreme Court make consideration of a similar case likely. In dissent, Justice Powell saw Washington's law as racially neutral and said that ". . . a decision *not* to assign students on the basis of race does not offend the 14th Amendment. The Court has never held that there is an affirmative duty to integrate the schools in the absence of a finding of unconstitutional segregation."[9]

What did Seattle do with its schools?

SINCE 1989, THE SEATTLE SCHOOL DISTRICT has tried to fashion a balance between two, sometimes conflicting, goals. On the one hand it must desegregate schools. On the other hand, it must allow parents and students some educational choices or risk losing them to private and suburban schools. The school board's solution has been to allow a limited choice where parents may select their first and second choices among a group of several schools. Elementary school students have a choice among the schools in their "cluster"; middle and high-school students pick a school from a "zone" (which is made up of several clusters). A school that everybody knows is unattractive is made less so by giving that school special programs. For example, a "magnet" school would be the only one in a cluster with a bilingual program or the only school that has a performing arts program.

Does Seattle's "Choices" program work?

YES. "CHOICES" has brought Seattle schools closer to meeting both desegregation and parental choice goals. In fact, desegregation has become somewhat easier as "magnet" schools tend naturally to draw students away from their neighborhoods.

The school district must still maintain racial percentage limits at schools, even with the "Choices" program. A school should not vary more than 20% from the minority percentage of population in the Seattle School District as a whole.

Therefore, to be within guidelines, a Seattle school must be somewhere between 30 and 70% minority. No school should be more than 70% White.

Within the limits of Seattle's "clusters' and "zones," 80% of parents/students get their first pick of schools. Those that do not get the desired school, can challenge the decision. The odds of winning an appeal are pretty good: 1/3 of written appeals are granted and 1/3 of heard appeals are granted.[10]

Other Schools and Other Choices

When may a student attend a technical college?

STARTING IN THE 11TH GRADE, or at the age of 16, students have the option of attending a vocational-technical school (or technical college) instead of a regular high school. As with public high schools, the student does not pay for attending these schools while he or she is of high-school age. However, the student is responsible for applying for admission to his or her new vocational school.[11]

Students always have the option of taking vocational courses at their own high school instead of switching to a technical college. The difference is one of depth. Washington's technical colleges offer 260 different training programs (from graphical artists to cooks) with the express purpose of getting students jobs immediately after graduation.

What are "alternative schools"?

ALTERNATIVE SCHOOLS ARE SMALLER, less-structured *public* schools. They offer the same curriculum as the standard school but usually offer little in the way of extra activities such as sports and clubs.

In the lower grades, alternative schools may teach students one-to-one, or in small groups, making extra efforts to respond to the individual student's academic *and* emotional needs. In the high school grades, alternative schools focus on students whose lives don't fit with the traditional school schedule. Perhaps the student is struggling to work half-time *and* complete school or get an equivalency diploma. Perhaps a student is a new parent. Alternative schools allow enough flexibility for these students to stay in school and graduate.

Where do alternative schools come from?

MOST OFTEN PARENTS OR TEACHERS create them. Of the state's 25 alternative elementary schools, most were started by parents who wanted to continue the pre-school format into grades 1-6. Parents liked the small, non-graded classes, the self-paced instruction, and their own participation in pre-school education and wanted to see those same practices in later grades.

Teachers most often start alternative secondary schools. They see a type of student that could use a special type of environment and decide to create a "pilot program." These experiments then spin off into full-fledged schools.

Whoever wants to form an alternative school must first objectively assess its need and purpose. Many questions need answers: What students will the school serve? Are there enough of them? What is the guiding idea behind the school's creation? How will students be taught? What is the place of parents in the new school? Once these questions are satisfactorily answered, then the school will receive traditional state funding and be under the supervision of the district school board.

What are the rules for private schools?

THE STATE "recognizes that private schools should be subject only to those minimum state controls necessary to insure the health and safety of all the students in the state and to insure a sufficient basic education to meet usual graduation requirements."[12] Legitimate private schools, like public schools, must have a 180-day school year. They must have certified teachers except for classes where no counterpart or similar course exists in the public schools. And private schools must provide sufficient instruction for students to meet the state board of education graduation requirements.

May parents educate their children at home?

YES. WASHINGTON STATE ALLOWS regulated home-based instruction, or "homeschooling." Parents qualify to teach their own children in at least one of three ways:
- the parent may complete a course on home-based education at a Washington college, university, or vocational school;
- the parent may be supervised by a certified teacher who helps plan and evaluate the parent's instruction; or,
- the local school district superintendent may decide the parent is qualified and waive the above requirements.[13]

What must parents teach when homeschooling?

THE STATE'S POSITION is that while parents have a right to guide their child's education, the state has a duty to see that the child *does*, in fact, receive a basic education. This being so, the state requires some regulation of content including "a curriculum and instruction in the basic skills of occupational education, science, mathematics, social studies, history, health, reading, writing, spelling, and the development of an appreciation of art and music."[14]

How this is done is a matter up to the parent, as home schooling does not have to follow a curriculum identical to that in the public schools. "Therefore, all decisions relating to philosophy or doctrine, selection of books, teaching materials and curriculum, and methods, timing, and place in the provision or evaluation of home-based instruction shall be the responsibility of the parent."[15]

May homeschoolers also attend public schools?

YES. SCHOOL DISTRICTS PERMIT home-based students to attend instructional courses *part-time.* Sometimes these students may also participate in public school sports, depending on the eligibility requirements outlined by the Washington Interscholastic Athletics Association. Public school transportation is also available to part-time students.[16]

Where do students go to school?

THE OVERWHELMING MAJORITY of Washington's 900,000 K-12 students attend public schools. The percentage that attends private schools has declined over the past decade and now stands at about 8%. It is difficult to determine the exact number of children in homeschooling. The state estimates around 7000, private school organizations put the number at about 10,000, and homeschooling organizations say as many as 20,000.[17] The difficulty is that parents don't have to notify the school district until the age of eight that their children will be in homeschooling.

11

Special Education

Is education provided for a handicapped child?

YES. "THE SUPERINTENDENT of public instruction shall require each school district in the state to insure an appropriate educational opportunity for all handicapped children between the ages of three and twenty-one."[18] As the State is constitutionally bound to provide "basic education" to all children, school districts receive funds just for special education programs.

The steady growth in handicapped (or special education) programs over the past decade is due to new governmental policies and not an increasing number of handicapped students.[19] Federal and state mandates for handicapped services have gone hand-in-hand with public awareness and concern for these students.[20]

How are students placed in special education?

IF PARENTS OR SCHOOL PERSONNEL think a child has a handicapped condition, then an "assessment process" determines what, if any, special education the child will receive. A group of qualified professionals, including at least one with specific knowledge in the student's suspected handicapped condition, examines the child's school and medical records as well as the reason for the referral.

Where are special education students placed?

SPECIAL EDUCATION STUDENTS must be educated with students who are not handicapped whenever possible. This "least restrictive environment" or "mainstreaming" policy means that the *student's needs* come first in determining placement, not other conditions (for example, whether or not there is classroom space). If the regular classroom would not work out, then the student may be able to attend special classes located at a regular school. For the severely handicapped, there are special residential schools, home or hospital instruction, or an education at an institution managed by the state's department of social and health services.

How can parents assist in special education?

PARENTS HAVE THE RIGHT to guide, participate in, and evaluate their child's special education program. Parents help develop their child's Individual Education Program (IEP) along side school district personnel. This includes setting and monitoring the student's educational goals, and then picking the right educational service to accomplish them.

If parents are unhappy with their child's special education, they can request mediation to answer their concerns. If that doesn't solve the problem, then a hearing is held to consider the original assessment, placement, or educational program of the student.

Discipline

Who can discipline a student?

TEACHERS, SCHOOL ADMINISTRATORS, and bus drivers may all discipline a student who violates school district rules. This includes the authority to have the disrupting or threatening student removed from an activity, class, or subject.[21]

How severely may officials punish a student?

DEPENDING ON HOW BADLY THE STUDENT BEHAVES and individual school rules, school districts may suspend a student for a short term (of up to five days), impose a long-term suspension, or expel the student from a particular class or even from school property. School personnel have a responsibility to try other ways of correcting the student's behavior, including other kinds of punishment, before these extreme measures are taken.

What are parental rights concerning discipline?

SCHOOLS MUST NOTIFY PARENTS of any type of student suspension over a day or of a child's expulsion. The more serious the discipline problem, the more involved and formal the process of deciding punishment. Parents have a right to a conference with the building's principal, the disciplining teacher, and the student to sort out the problem and discuss how to prevent it from happening again. Parents and/or students may appeal what they consider an unfair expulsion or suspension.

Is corporal punishment allowed?

YES. "CORPORAL PUNISHMENT consisting of spanking or striking a student shall be administered only in an office or some other area outside the view of [their] students and only by an authorized employee in the presence of and witnessed by another school district employee."[22]

While state law permits bodily punishment, it also discourages it and sets several restrictions on its use. Only moderate force may be used and certainly no form of cruel or unusual punishment is allowable. Only those teachers or administrators who have been authorized, in advance, by the child's parents, may inflict any sort of physical punishment. Parents may also request a written explanation of why their child was so punished.

Student Rights and Responsibilities

What are a student's rights?

- NO STUDENT SHALL BE UNLAWFULLY DENIED an equal educational opportunity or be unlawfully discriminated against because of national origin, race, religion, economic status, sex, pregnancy, marital status, previous arrest, previous incarceration, or a physical, mental, or sensory handicap.
- All students possess the constitutional right to freedom of speech and press, the constitutional right to peaceably assemble and to petition the government and its representatives for a redress of grievances, the constitutional right to the free exercise of religion and to have their schools free from sectarian control or influence, subject to reasonable limitations upon the time, place, and manner of exercising such right.
- All students possess the constitutional right to be secure in their persons, papers, and effects against unreasonable searches and seizures.
- No student shall be deprived of the right to an equal educational opportunity in whole or in part by a school district without due process of law.
- All students shall have the right to be free from unlawful interference in their pursuit of an education while in the custody of a common school district.[23]

What are the responsibilities of a student?

EVERY SCHOOL DISTRICT is to have a document listing the rules and regulations concerning student conduct. These rules, and disciplinary procedures, are available to every student, their parents, and teachers. "All pupils who attend the common schools shall comply with the rules and regulations established in pursuance of the law for the government of the schools, shall pursue the required course of studies, and shall submit to the authority of the teachers of such schools, subject to such disciplinary or other action as the local school officials determine."[24]

What is the Buckley Amendment?

IN 1974, THE UNITED STATES CONGRESS passed the Family Educational Rights and Privacy Act (FERPA), commonly known as the Buckley Amendment. This law defines who may and may not see a student's school record. The intent of the law is to ensure that all student records contain only objective information directly relevant to the student's education.

Do parents have access to a child's record?

YES. FEDERAL LAW GUARANTEES FIVE parental rights concerning student records.

• School districts must have a written policy regarding access to all the information they collect concerning a particular student. Parents must be informed yearly about this policy.
• Parent have the right to inspect their child's student record

and obtain an explanation of what is in it and why it is there.

• There must be a procedure to challenge the accuracy of a child's student record.

• Parents must give their consent for release of any information from the student record to outsiders. This does not include basic biographical information such as the student's name and address, and school activities. Schools must keep a record of who requests access to a student's record.

• Parents may file complaints with a FERPA office if they feel a school has failed to comply with the above laws.

How do parents challenge a record's accuracy?

IF, AFTER INSPECTION OF THEIR CHILD'S student record, parents consider it wrong or misleading, then they may request a hearing to correct the record. In the hearing, evidence will be presented on both sides of the question. If the parents are right, then the record will be amended. If not, the parents may have their objection included as part of their child's permanent student record.[25]

May a student see his or her own record?

STUDENTS THEMSELVES OBTAIN THE RIGHTS of their parents when they turn 18 or start attending college.

Do students have a right to free speech?

YES. THEY HAVE A RIGHT to free expression in the classroom, anywhere on the school grounds, and at school activities. In 1969, several high-school students from Des Moines, Iowa, wore black armbands to school to protest the Vietnam War. School officials, who had been alerted to this possibility, had recently passed a rule disallowing such an act because of the trouble it could cause. They suspended the students on the grounds of that policy. The children's parents took the case to court, arguing that the rights of the students to express themselves overrode the school rules to keep order.

The United States Supreme Court sided with the parents. "Any word spoken in class, in the lunchroom, or on the campus that deviates from the views of another person may start an argument or cause a disturbance. But our Constitution says we must take this risk; and our history says that it is this sort of hazardous freedom — this kind of openness — that is the basis of our national strength and of the independence and vigor of Americans who grow up and live in this relatively permissive, often disputatious society. In our system, students may not be regarded as closed-circuit recipients of only what the State chooses to communicate."[26] If protesting students interfere with the other students' education or security, then the school may restrain their activity.

Is there a limit to students' free speech?

YES. ALL CONSTITUTIONAL RIGHTS have their limitations. At Bethel High School (Pierce County), a student delivered a nomination speech, full of sexual metaphors, to a school assembly. The speech caused some students to be disruptive while others became embarrassed. The student, who had been forewarned by teachers that the speech was inappropriate, was suspended for two days. The student sued the school district on the grounds that his free speech rights were violated by the punishment.

The United States Supreme Court disagreed. Schools can limit lewd and indecent speech because it seriously undermines their educational mission. This student simply went too far.[27] The decision read in part: "The undoubted freedom to advocate unpopular and controversial views in schools and classrooms must be balanced against the countervailing interest in teaching students the boundaries of socially acceptable behavior."[28]

Are student newspapers part of the free press?

NO. STUDENT RIGHTS ARE NOT ALWAYS EQUAL to adult rights in other settings. In particular, a student newspaper is under some restrictions that cannot be imposed on a private company's paper.

As part of a journalism class, students wrote two controversial articles for their newspaper *The Spectrum*. One article was about three students' experiences before and during their pregnancies. Another article was about the impact on a student when her parent's divorced. The principal stopped the publication of the articles on the grounds that (a) the students written about could be identified from the articles (b) the first article was too explicit for younger students and (c) the article on divorce did not include the parents response to their child's comments.

The Supreme Court took the principal's side in the matter. "Educators are entitled to exercise greater control [over student's public written work] of student expression to assure that participants learn whatever lessons the school is designed to teach, that readers are not exposed to materials that may be inappropriate for their level of maturity and that the views of the individual speakers are not erroneously attributed to the school."[29] In general, the court does not see a school as a

19

completely open forum with all the rights of adult political debate. Unlike personal student speech, the newspaper was essentially part of the school curriculum and so it was reasonable that the teacher or administrator would exercise some discrimination over content.

Dissenting judges said the majority decision taught the students a poor civics lesson in the rights of free expression. The controversial articles did not interfere with other student's education or security and there was no reason to pull them. These justices ended with a question: Were the articles pulled because of their subject or the viewpoint?

Are "dress codes" legal?

SOMETIMES. Most schools have some sort of dress code although it is more likely to deal with acceptable clothing than grooming decision such as hair length. The courts have decided, at one time or another, both ways on this issue. On the side of students challenging dress codes, the courts recognize that student dress is a matter of personal freedom and does not hurt any other student's education. On the other hand, the courts recognize that schools want to have dress codes to avoid the disruptions and distractions caused by strange dress.

The Ninth District Court of Appeals, which handles Washington cases, has upheld school dress code policies in recent years. The United States Supreme Court has not entered the disputes, considering them a trivial concern. In rejecting an appeal in a dress code case, Justice Black wrote: "The only thing about this that borders on the serious to me is that anyone should think the Federal Constitution imposes on the United States courts the burden of supervising the length of hair the public school students should wear." [30]

Do military recruiters have competition?

SOME SCHOOL DISTRICTS THINK THEY SHOULD. "Equal Access" to high school students is then given to military recruiters *and* various peace groups. The reasoning is that all sides of military life should be presented. Military recruiters promote the educational and career benefits of the military and the chance to act on one's patriotism. Peace activists question the military's promises of paying for a full college education and supplying worthwhile training. They also contend that there is an overemphasis on the military in United States foreign policy.[31]

The military does not have a problem with equal access. There are several reasons for this. Operation Desert Storm has resulted in more and better recruits; the new enlistee is as interested in a military career for patriotic reasons as much as for job opportunities. Also, the United States armed forces are shrinking and that means recruiters can be picky; they recruit graduating high school seniors only. So far, they have no problem in attracting some 3000 Washington graduates to the Army, Navy, Air Force, Marines, and Coast Guard each year.[32]

Is sexual equality a student right?

YES. THERE MUST BE NO INEQUALITY in the educational opportunities offered to students.[33]

- All classes and courses must be open to both sexes (with the exception of gym and sex education classes).
- Guidance counselors stress that all career and vocational paths are open to both female and male students.
- Schools may field separate male and female sports

teams, but must provide each with equal equipment, medical care, transportation, coaching, and use of facilities. However, if the public and student interest in one team is obviously greater, then school officials may give that team a better, or more convenient game time.

What are the rights of pregnant students?

SCHOOLS MUST NOT DISCRIMINATE against pregnant students or teen parents in general. Federal law Title IX requires schools to allow pregnant teens (and student-fathers) to participate in all school clubs, classes, and within reason, sports. Young mothers return to school when their doctor recommends it, not according to a school-imposed time-table or regulation.

Teen pregnancy is a major problem in Washington. One in twelve adolescent girls become pregnant and of those pregnancies, one in three is a repeat pregnancy. Of the 15,518 teen pregnancies in 1989, 8,052 girls gave live births and 7,466 had abortions. One mother in forty puts her baby up for adoption.[34]

Students Needing Extra Help

What about students needing extra help?

WASHINGTON STATE HAS ITS OWN Learning Assistance Program (LAP) to help those students with learning problems and poor academic performance. The goal of the program is to help these "children at risk" at the earliest possible grade within the regular classroom. Each school district participating in the learning assistance program must continually assess the need for such a program and plan how to identify those students needing help. Parents and school officials make up an advisory committee to monitor learning assistance programs in their school district.[35]

What happens in learning assistance programs?

EACH SCHOOL DISTRICT TAILORS its learning assistance program a little differently. There are a variety of approaches that schools might choose to try:

- schools hire consultant teachers and support staff to assist regular classroom teachers;
- teachers receive special training to identify and address students with learning problems;
- tutoring is made available during the school day or outside of normal school hours; and,
- parents themselves take some training classes to help their child learn.

Who else helps slow learners?

THE FEDERAL GOVERNMENT has two programs titled "Chapter 1" and "Chapter 2" that operate alongside the state's learning assistance programs. These federal programs stress helping the poorer students in the poorer school districts.[36]

Both state and federal programs stress keeping those students who need extra help in the regular classroom by having one-to-one tutoring and smaller "classes within classes." These methods prevent a slower student from being unnecessarily side-tracked into a special education class.

Is bilingual education a right?

YES. WASHINGTON STATE IS CONSTITUTIONALLY BOUND to ensure equal protection opportunities and so provides for "transitional" bilingual education programs in all school districts. Bilingual education is "transitional" in that two languages are used, the child's first language, say Spanish, is used as a bridge to English. School districts must determine those students with the greatest need for bilingual education, and by testing them at the end of each year, measure their progress towards learning English. When a bilingual student scores in the 35th percentile in a Reading and Language Arts test, he or she leaves the program.

Is bilingual education successful?

SOMEWHAT. Of the roughly 25,000 bilingual students in Washington State, 11% a year pass the English language proficiency test and leave the program. Another 14% take over three years to pass the test and 18% quit the program in the first year. The most common languages are by far Spanish, Vietnamese, and Cambodian. The school districts with the most bilingual students are Seattle, Pasco, Yakima, and Tacoma.[37]

Dropouts

What are schools doing to prevent dropouts?

THE STATE ENCOURAGES SCHOOL DISTRICTS to develop innovative programs to stop students from dropping out of school. The state helps pay for such programs, especially in those districts with a proven pattern of high dropout rates. Schools want these dropouts back. To help them return, students who have dropped out of school for over six weeks, teen parents, and those students who stopped school to seek drug or mental treatment may all return to *any* high school in the state. [38]

Do dropout prevention programs work?

NOT REALLY. The percentage of students dropping out before graduation has remained about the same over the past six years. An annual dropout rate of 6% a year, starting in the 9th grade, means a cumulative class loss of 24% before graduation.[39]

One exception is the new SMART program. It identifies potential dropouts and enrolls them for eight weeks of summer school at a college campus. Along with classes, the students work at university science labs and on community projects. The change of environment seems to do the students good — so far, all the SMART participants have stayed in school.

What can a dropout do to finish school?

ONE PATH A DROPOUT CAN CHOOSE TO FOLLOW is to attend one of the over twenty "educational clinics" in this state. Educational clinics are private schools where certified teachers focus on a student's specific educational needs. If accepted by the clinic, the student's tuition is paid by the state.

Students at educational clinics proceed at their own pace and not necessarily in a program shaped by high school requirements and schedules. The goal is simple: have these students return to school, get a GED, or find useful employment.

What about the GED test?

STUDENTS WHO FINISH THEIR INDIVIDUAL PROGRAM at an educational clinic are eligible to take the General Educational Development test as are those students who have a "substantial and warranted reason for leaving the regular high school program." If a student's parents agree, the student may leave the regular high school program for either personal problems or to seek viable employment, or to join the military.[40] . Students who receive at least an average score of at least 45/100 on the GED are eligible for a Certificate of Educational Competence from the Superintendent of Public Instruction.

Adults who never finished high school are also encouraged to study and take the GED. In fact, of the roughly 11,000 GEDs awarded each year, most by far are to adults .[41]

Programs For Exceptional Students

What is there for "highly capable" students?

THE STATE RECOGNIZES THAT STUDENTS with exceptional intellectual and/or creative ability need special programs that allow them to learn at their own rate. Such programs exist for students to reach their full potential and assume responsibility for their own education. The state's goal is to eventually include the top 3% of all students in these programs. Parents, teachers, and students may nominate someone for a highly capable student program. Determining who is accepted is not just a matter of opinion. Students should meet one of these three criteria:

- score in the top 10% in cognitive ability on a standard ability test;
- score in the top 5% in one or more specific academic achievement tests; or
- show exceptional creativity in their school work.[42]

In general, the best programs for gifted children are found in elementary and secondary schools. Middle school, or Junior High programs are less developed and less focused.[43]

What are some gifted-student programs?

•THE PENINSULA SCHOOL DISTRICT (Pierce County) with roughly 7000 students has a variety of gifted children programs. The Odyssey of the Mind program has specialists visiting each elementary school once a week for special classes with the best students. "Community mentors" also visit school after-hours for extra study in foreign languages, art, and computers. At the secondary level, advanced students may a get "running start" at higher education by attending some community college courses during the regular school day.

•Republic School District (Ferry County) is a medium-sized district (600 students) that has a pull-out program (students leave the classroom) for 4th through 6th graders. This year students are building their own fossil collections, and each will present his or her finding to the class as a whole. In another project, gifted children have their own projects in investigating water quality and reporting back to the class. Sixteen students participate in the program.

•Most of the smaller school districts also have some sort of special consideration for the most talented children. The

Steptoe School District (Whitman County) has only 40 students but gives some of them extra computer time. The Quilcene School District (Jefferson County), with 270 students, allows the best students from a lower grade to spend part of their class time with students from higher grades.

How can parents help with these programs?

PARENTS ARE ENCOURAGED TO JOIN or form groups within a local school district that support programs for highly capable students. They can donate their particular skills or professional talents to such programs. Parents who are members of the Northwest Gifted Children Association may bring ideas from the organization to their own group.

NOTES

[1] RCW 28A.225.010.
[2] RCW 28A.225.020, RCW 28A.225.030.
[3] RCW 28A.225.090.
[4] RCW 28A.600.030.
[5] WAC 392-137-135.
[6] Ramsdell v. North River School District Wn.2d 264 (1985).
[7] By December of 1991, parents will receive the details of the state's Choice plan from their children's school.
[8] Washington v. Seattle School District 102 S.Ct 3187 (1987)
[9] Same case as above.
[10] From Seattle School District A&S Center.
[11] RCW 28A.600.310.
[12] RCW 28A.195.010.
[13] RCW 28A,225.010(4).
[14] RCW 28A.225.010(4).

[15]   RCW 28A.200.020.

[16]   RCW 28A.150.350.

[17]   1991 estimate from Washington Federation of Independent Schools.

[18]   RCW 28A.155.020.

[19]   Handicapped enrollment is now at 85,000 or 9.8% of kindergarten through 12th grade enrollment. *Public Schools K-12 and Handicapped Enrollment Forecasts 1991-1993 Budget* State Office of Financial Management.

[20]   Parents of handicapped children should get the state's booklet *Guide to Special Education in Washington.*

[21]   WAC 180-40-230.

[22]   WAC 180-40-245(3).

[23]   WAC 180-40-215.

[24]   RCW 28A.600.040.

[25]   For a full explanation on student records, see *Parents, Schools, and the Law* (1987) by Daniel Schimmel and Louis Fischer.

[26]   Tinker v. Des Moines Independent School District 393 U.S. 503 (1969) The First Amendment of the United States Constitution: "Congress shall make no law respecting an establishment of religion, or prohibiting the free exercise thereof; or abridging the freedom of speech, or of the press; or the right of the people peaceably to assemble, and to petition the Government for a redress of grievances."

[27]   The full text of the speech: "I know a man who is firm - he's firm in his pants, he's firm in his shirt, his character is firm - but . . . most of all, his belief in you, the students of Bethel, is firm. [student] is a man who takes his point and pounds it in. If necessary, he'll take and nail it to the wall. He doesn't attack things in spurts - he drives hard, pushing and pushing until, finally, he succeeds. [student] is a man who will go to the very end, even the climax, for each and every one of you. So vote for [student] for ASB Vice-President - he'll never come between you and the best our high school can be."

[28]   Bethel School District v. Fraser 106 S.Ct 3159 (1986).

[29]   Hazelwood School District v. Kuhlmeier 108 S.Ct 562 (1988).

[30]   Karr v. Schmidt 401 U.S. 1201 (1971).

[31]   National Public Radio, Morning Edition, KPLU (May 1, 1991).

[32]   From Bill Pearce, Public Affairs Specialist, Seattle Army Recruiting Battalion (May 10, 1991).

[33]   Washington State Constitution, Article XXXI, Section 1, Amendment 61 "Equality of rights and responsibility shall not be denied or abridged on account of sex". Applied to the public schools through RCW 28A.640.

[34] From Washington Alliance Concerned With School Age Pregnancy.

[35] RCW 28A.165.010.

[36] "Chapter 1 Migrant" helps the children of migrant farms workers with the Migrant Student Record Transfer System, a computer system that keeps track of students as they move from school to school and from state to state.

[37] *Washington State Transitional Bilingual Instruction Program End-of-year Evaluation Report 1989-1990* Office of the Superintendent for Public Instruction.

[38] RCW 28A.175.090.

[39] To determine the exact dropout rate more information is necessary. The Office of the Superintendent of Public Instruction defines a dropout as a student who leaves school for any reason. But some students complete their GED soon after quitting school. If the 18 and 19 year-olds who obtain GEDs are not counted as dropouts, the state's overall dropout rate may be around 20%.

[40] WAC 180-96-045.

[41] *Dropout Rates and Graduation Statistics By County and School District For School Year 1988-89* Office of the Superintendent for Public Instruction.

[42] Interested parents should obtain the state's booklet *Programs For Highly Capable Students*.

[43] Phil Sorensen, Gifted Programs, Puget Sound Educational Service District.

Part II. Teachers

Hiring and Qualifications

Who is hired to teach?

TO RECEIVE AN INITIAL TEACHING CERTIFICATE in Washington State, all applicants must meet the following eight qualifications:

- earned a bachelor's degree from a regionally accredited college;
- present a transcript of their college courses;
- completed a teacher education program approved by the State Board of Education;
- completed 30 semester hours in a major "endorsement area" (for example: Early Childhood Education for Preschool-3rd grade or Biology for 4-12th grade teacher);
- taken a course in child abuse issues;
- present evidence of good moral character with three character references;
- present verification of good standing for teaching certificates held in other states; and,
- verify through Washington State Patrol that he or she has no criminal history.

Do teachers have to take competency tests?

NO. HOWEVER, TO ATTEND A TEACHING COLLEGE, aspiring teachers must be in the upper half of their class (as measured by a score above the state-wide median on a standardized test).

Also, starting in 1993, prospective teachers will be required to pass a uniform, "exit examination" before completing their college training program and the initial teaching certificate. This new essay examination will test new teachers' instructional skills, classroom management, and knowledge of student behavior and development.[1]

There are no further tests once a teacher receives his or her initial certificate.

Who else is permitted to teach?

SCHOOL DISTRICTS MAY HIRE EXPERTS or professionals to teach a special course for a limited time. The Teaching Specialist Certificates are also called "Einstein Certificates" because before this type of certificate, Albert Einstein could not have taught physics in Washington's public schools unless he had proof no one else was qualified. Continued high growth in enrollment, a shortage of teachers, and the opportunity to bring in new creative talent caused the State Board of Education to create this new type of certification.

There is also an Internship Teaching Certificate that permits mid-career persons who switch to teaching to start right away. Applicants must have a bachelor's degree and at least five years of work experience. Accepted teachers must then take evening and summer courses towards their teaching degree while starting work within the classroom.

How do teachers remain certified?

EXPERIENCED TEACHERS POSSESS CONTINUING CERTIFICATES that are renewed every five years. To stay certified, these teachers need 150 clock hours (or 10 college semester hours) of "in-service" training every five years.[2] "In-service" training does not have to consist of college courses; credit is also obtained from lectures and seminars organized at the district level. For example, a district may bring in a specialist in teaching writing for a seminar with English teachers. Or a teacher most knowledgeable about computers may instruct her colleagues on using computers. Teachers must only attend 'in-service" training in courses directly related to their daily classroom instruction

Salaries

Who determines teacher salaries?

THE STATE LEGISLATURE DETERMINES TEACHER SALARIES in its biennial budget. The state-wide percentage increase works as a cap for the amount of money a school district receives for teacher salaries. School districts do have some leeway in dividing up their salary allocation. For example, if the state allocates teachers a 5% raise, not all teachers have to receive exactly 5%; one group of teachers of similar education and experience could receive a 7% raise as long as another group received a 3% raise to balance things out. Of course, most districts have collective bargaining agreements with teachers that limit how school boards distribute the state's lump-sum salary allocation.

In 1991, the minimum starting teacher salary is $20,801 with a bachelor's degree or $24,939 for a starting teacher with a master's degree. The base salary is $41,159 for a teacher with 15 years experience and 135 credit hours. These salaries will go up 3.5% in 1992.

Are teachers paid the same across the state?

ALMOST ALWAYS TEACHERS OF EQUAL EXPERIENCE and education are paid the same across the state. There are some districts, (for example, Everett), that are not completely on the state salary schedule. There is no adjustment to take into account the cost of living difference between geographical areas although studies show teacher salaries in the Puget Sound area amount to 25% less in purchasing power compared to those east of the Cascades.[3]

There is some movement to change the salary structure to equate equal work with equal purchasing power, not straight salary. There is also a reluctance to pay some teachers more because they choose to live in wealthier school districts.

In the Classroom

What are a teacher's duties?

STATE LAW LISTS SEVERAL general job requirements for a teacher:

• Implement the district's prescribed curriculum and enforce, within their area of responsibility, the rules and regulations of the school district, the state superintendent of public instruction, and the state board of education, taking into consideration individual differences among students;

• Maintain good order and discipline in their classroom at all times;

• Hold students to a strict accountability while in school for any disorderly conduct while under their supervision;

• Require excuses from the parents in all cases of absence, late arrival to school, or early dismissal;

- Give careful attention to the maintenance of a healthful atmosphere in the classroom;
- Give careful attention to the safety of the student in the classroom and report any doubtful or unsafe conditions to the building administrator; and,
- Evaluate each student's educational growth and development and make periodic reports thereon to parents.[4]

How many students may be in a teacher's class?

THERE IS NO SET LIMIT on the number of students in a particular class. Instead, the state funds school districts to hire enough certified staff to meet state guidelines for *average* class size. In 1991, for Kindergarten through 3rd grade, these averages are 1 certified staff for every 18.5 students. The averages are 1 certified staff for every 21.7 students in grades 4th through 12th grade. "Certified staff" *does not* include school administrators but *does* include non-classroom support staff such as librarians, counselors, and nurses.

Do teachers control what and how they teach?

NOT COMPLETELY. Schools and teachers have a legal responsibility to "implement the district's curriculum."[5] If an instructor's classroom method and course content are substantially different from the required course description, then the teacher will have to change.

Two teachers at an Everett high school (Snohomish County) taught a history course titled "Global Studies." Their classroom method stressed individual study and separate research and writing projects. When the school administrators did not renew the course after a "pilot program," the teachers sued on the grounds that their rights of academic freedom had been violated. The Washington Supreme Court disagreed: "While teachers should have some measure of freedom in teaching techniques employed, they may not ignore or omit essential course material or disregard the course calendar."[6] In this case, the "Global Studies" course was so different in teaching method that it differed in content and coverage as well. The Everett school board was justified in demanding some conformity in what was taught and how it was taught.

Out of School

May teachers publicly criticize school policies?

YES. SCHOOL BOARDS CANNOT PUNISH TEACHERS for speaking out by firing them or forcing them to transfer to another school or district.

A high school teacher wrote a long letter to the local newspaper concerning a proposed tax increase for the schools. Among the charges were that the school board deceived the taxpayers on how school funds were spent and that excessive spending on athletics took money away from insufficient teacher salaries. The school board fired the teacher because the letter was "detrimental to the efficient operation and administration of the school and the district." The teacher sued on grounds that the letter was protected under the First Amendment. The United States Supreme Court heard the case to clarify the "balance between the interests of the teacher, as a citizen, in commenting upon matters of public concern and the interest of the State, as an employer, in promoting the efficiency of the public services it performs through its employees."

The court sided with the teacher: "The question whether a school system requires additional funds is a matter of legitimate public concern on which the matter of the school administration, including the School Board, cannot, in a society that leaves such questions open to popular vote, be taken as conclusive. Teachers are, as a class, the members of the community most likely to be informed, and have definite opinions as to how funds allotted to the operation of the schools be spent. Accordingly, it is essential that they be able to speak out freely on such questions without fear of retaliatory dismissal."[7]

What if a teacher's criticisms are untrue?

IF THE TEACHER MADE STATEMENTS he or she knew were false or if the teacher made no effort to discover the truth, then he or she may be dismissed. Even then, the school administration must show that the comments were damaging to school operations.

Teachers may also be dismissed for obvious slander, betraying confidential conversations that hurt the schools, or revealing personal information about students. These things have no bearing on public policy and undermine a school system.

Who represents teacher interests?

LOCAL AFFILIATES OF THE WASHINGTON Education Association (WEA) represent almost all of the state's kindergarten through 12th grade teachers. Members of each local affiliate pick representatives to negotiate a 1-3 year contract with the local school district. Up for negotiation are the teachers' work environment, hours, salary schedule, and overtime regulations. The negotiators may choose to call on the help of UniServ, a National Education Association (NEA) program that provides organizing and bargaining support to local collective bargaining efforts. WEA membership also serves teachers by covering members with $1 million in liability protection as well as providing various insurance policies.

Must teachers join a union?

No, BUT USUALLY THEY MUST PAY UNION DUES. Most of Washington's school districts have "agency shop" or "fair share" contracts with the local affiliate of the WEA. In those situations, employees that choose not to join the union are still required to pay dues as a condition of employment. The reason behind this is that the union's collective bargaining benefits all teachers so the cost should be shared by all.

Union dues are about $450 a year with $100 to the NEA (national level), $200 to the WEA (state level), $50 to UniServ (regional level), and $100 to the local (district) affiliate.

Non-members, and those members that take the option, do not have to pay the $15 per year cost of the Washington Education Association's political activities (such as the political action committee PULSE — Political Unity of Leaders in State Education).[8]

What are the union's goals?

THE WEA'S REPRESENTATIVE ASSEMBLY has adopted three main goals for the organization:[9]

- increase money in the system to fund schools, decrease class size, improve the retirement system and increase salaries;
- become a powerful and constructive force for excellence and equity in the educational decision-making systems in Washington; and,
- restore free and open collective bargaining and local decision making.

Evaluation

How are teachers evaluated?

PRINCIPALS EVALUATE TEACHERS on "instructional skill, classroom management, professional preparation and scholarship; effort toward improvement when needed; the handling of student discipline and attendant problems; and interest in teaching pupils and knowledge of subject matter."[10]

During the first four years of a teacher's career, the principal evaluates the instructor twice a year for at least an hour of total observation time. Following each observation period, the principal (or another *trained* evaluator) writes up an evaluation and provides a copy to the teacher. For teachers with more than four years experience, the school district may choose a policy of shorter observation periods for two years and the full evaluation every three years. Teachers also have the opportunity to discuss their work privately with their immediate supervisor twice a year.

Washington teachers are on probation for one year before receiving tenure. Once a teacher has tenure, he or she cannot be discharged quickly without full due process rights.

Who evaluates a teacher's evaluator?

PRINCIPALS EVALUATE THEIR DIRECT SUBORDINATES; local superintendents evaluate principals. Evaluation criteria depend on the administrator's exact position but always include "knowledge of, experience in, and training in recognizing good professional performance, effort toward improvement when needed, interest in pupils, employees, patrons, and subjects taught in school, leadership and ability and performance of school personnel."[11] Administrators receiving poor job reviews may be transferred to a subordinate position by the superintendent. While the disciplined administrator has a right to a hearing, there is no required probation period similar to that for teachers.[12]

How is a teacher found incompetent?

WHEN AN EVALUATOR FINDS a teacher's classroom performance unsatisfactory, the teacher may be placed on probation from February through May. The principal and teacher will create an improvement program for the teacher to follow. Observation and continued evaluation increase during that probation period. If the teacher does not improve during probation then, by May 15, the superintendent may choose to fire the teacher if that is the recommendation of the teacher's evaluator.[13]

The discharged teacher may request a hearing to challenge the decision. If so, a hearing must be held, where the teacher defends his or her record and challenges the fairness of his or her release. Both the teacher and the school district may subpoena witnesses and take pre-hearing depositions to support their position. Only tenured teachers (those teaching at least 1 year) receive this full procedure.

What is at issue when a teacher is discharged?

TWO FACTORS DETERMINE whether a teacher's conduct warrants dismissal. The first is to verify that the *facts* of the situation, as observed by the evaluator and others are true. The second is to determine that there is *"sufficient cause"* to let the teacher go. A "remedial teaching deficiency" that the teacher may correct in time does not constitute "sufficient cause."

In a Shoreline school district (King County) case, the teacher could not locate students or materials because of sight and hearing problems; he also had trouble controlling students and had poorly prepared or non-existent lesson plans. The teacher was put on probation and eventually discharged after refusing to shift to a non-teaching job. The courts stood by the school district's original decision to let the teacher go. The district proved the teacher broke district rules, jeopardized student safety, and had problems that were basically uncorrectable.[14]

What is "sufficient cause" to fire a teacher?

THE SHORELINE CASE DECISION listed several "ground rules" for determining "sufficient cause." In the event that a teacher challenges his or her dismissal in the courts, several points will be considered in the courts:
- the age and maturity of the students;
- the degree to which the teacher's conduct adversely affected students or other teachers;
- the proximity or remoteness in time of the teacher's conduct;
- the extenuating circumstances surrounding the teacher's conduct; and,
- the possibly chilling effect on the rights of teachers.

May teachers be dismissed for outside conduct?

NOT ALWAYS. A shop teacher at Mount Vernon high school (Skagit County) was fired when he was charged and convicted for purchasing a stolen motorcycle. The instructor, as was his right, appealed the school board decision to the Superior Court. That court agreed with the district that the teacher's conduct was "inherently harmful to the student-teacher relationship." Higher courts had the teacher reinstated, reasoning that the conviction did not *automatically* make a teacher unfit.[15] Although the lower court's punishment stood, the higher court found that the teacher taught competently and had the support of students and parent that doubted his guilt.

Of course, any teacher guilty of moral misconduct, such as sexual relations with a student, or drug use, will be dismissed and barred from teaching in this state.[16]

What rewards are there for the best teachers?

EVERY YEAR 40 TEACHERS RECEIVE Washington's Excellence in Education award, also known as the Christa McAuliffe Award (in honor of the teacher-astronaut killed on board the Challenger, January 28, 1986). The Governor and the Superintendent of Public Instruction present winning teachers with a certificate and an academic grant to be used for the teacher's own education. The Christa McAuliffe Award is a peer award; that is, only fellow teachers and principals, but not parents, nominate a colleague.[17]

Parent-Teacher Relations

May parents visit their child's class?

YES. "EVERY SCHOOL DISTRICT BOARD OF DIRECTORS shall, after following established procedure, adopt a policy assuring parents access to their child's classroom and/or school sponsored activities for purposes of observing class procedure, teaching material, and class conduct. Provided: That such observations shall not disrupt the classroom procedure or learning activity."[18]

What if parents are unhappy with a teacher?

PARENTS SHOULD TALK TO THE TEACHER. While parents do not have a right to choose their child's teacher, they have every right to let their other concerns be known. If meeting and talking with the teacher do not satisfy the parents, they may bring their concern to the school principal and then to the local superintendent. The school board is not the first place to go, but eventually it has responsibility to resolve disputes among parents, teachers, and students.

Extra Duties

What do teachers do if they suspect child abuse?

TAKE ACTION. IF TEACHERS, AND OTHER SCHOOL STAFF, have "reasonable cause to believe that a child or adult dependent or developmentally disabled person has suffered abuse or neglect, he or she shall report such incident, or cause a report to be made, to the proper law enforcement agency or to the department [of social and health services]. The report shall be made at the first opportunity, but in no case longer than forty-eight hours after there is reasonable cause to believe that the child or adult has suffered abuse or neglect."[19]

Parents should be aware that they have full due process rights when state agencies investigate child abuse cases. Nevertheless, top priority remains the protection of the potentially abused child.

What if the teacher is wrong about the abuse?

IF THE TEACHER'S REPORT OF CHILD ABUSE is made in good faith, then the teacher has nothing to fear from angry parents who may sue for character defamation. The school district must, in fact, provide for the legal defense of its employee.[20]

How are teachers responsible for student safety?

TEACHERS ALWAYS HAVE A RESPONSIBILITY to take care of their students. In a broad sense, this means warning students about foreseeable dangers in the classroom, in the gym, and on any sort of field trip. It certainly means teaching students about the proper use of any equipment they may use. Taking into account the grade and general experience of her students, the teacher must simply use good judgment about his or her students' safety. It does not mean the teacher has to be with his or her class at every moment (although someone of authority must be), but rather at all times when conditions are potentially dangerous.

When is a teacher liable for a student's

A STUDENT OR PARENTS MUST PROVE FOUR THINGS teacher guilty of negligence:[21]
- that in the situation where the student was in teacher had a duty to take "reasonable care" of the
- that the teacher failed to take reasonable care
- that the teacher's carelessness caused the stud injury, and that the student did not cause his or he injury; and,
- that the student was indeed injured.

These two cases illustrate how a court will probably at a teacher negligence case.

A teacher took a class of 8th grade girls out to the scho playing fields. She then left them to wait on a bench by baseball field while she returned to the building. As the waited, several boys playing baseball began throwing pebble at the girls. The girls warned them to stop, the boys didn't, and in time one of the girl's eyes was seriously injured. The court agreed with the parents when they sued on the grounds of negligence. The court thought it was reasonable for the teacher to have foreseen this conflict; it did not happen unexpectedly and was poor judgement on the teacher's part to leave the girls in jeopardy. [22]

In another out-of-state case, two teachers took a class of fifty 12-15 year olds on a field trip to a museum. When one of the boys was away from the group, he was beaten up by some boys not connected with the school. The boy's parents sued, claiming the teachers were negligent in supervision. The parents did not win in court. The judge thought there wasn't much risk of what happened at the museum. The teachers could not be held responsible for seeing every potential conflict. The court also noted that the constant supervision required to prevent that kind of accident would prevent schools from ever doing any sort of field trip. "To require round-the-clock supervision or prison-tight security for school premises would impose too great a financial burden on the school."[23]

NOTES

[1]   RCW 28A.410.020.

[2]   WAC 180-85-030, WAC 180-85-075.

[3]   *Is Fairness Served by Providing Equal Salary Allocation for Educators Across Washington?* by Neil D. Theobald , Puget Sound Educational Consortium.

[4]   RCW 28A.150.240(2).

[5]   RCW 28A.150.240.

[6]   Millikan v. Everett School District 93 Wn.2d 522 (1980).

[7]   Pickering v. Board of Education 88 S.Ct 1731 (1968).

[8]   The WEA has about 43, 000 members. Another 1000 teachers pay the dues but are not WEA members.

[9]   *The Association at a Glance 1990-91* The Washington Education Association.

[10]   RCW 28A.405.100.

[11]   RCW 28A.405.100(2).

[12]   RCW 28A.405.230. Also see Benson v. Bellevue School District Wn.App 730 (1985).

[13]   RCW 28A.405.100.

[14]   Clarke v. Shoreline School District 106 Wn.2d 102 (1986).

[15]   Hoagland v. Mount Vernon School District 95 Wn.2d 424 (1981).

[16]   This occurred 28 times in 1990. Office of Professional Practices Annual Report, January 1991, Office of the Superintendent of Public Instruction.

[17]   RCW 28.625. 5 administrators, 1 superintendent, 1 school board, and 24 classified school employees are also awarded each year.

[18]   RCW 28A.605.020.

[19]   RCW 26.44.030.

[20]   RCW 26.44.032.

[21]   *Teachers and the Law* (1981) by Louis Fisher, David Schimmel, and Cynthia Kelly Chapter "When Am I Liable."

[22]   Sheehan v. St Peter Catholic School, 188 N.W.2d 868 (1971).

[23]   Mancha v. Field Museum of Natural History, 283 N.E. 899 (Ill. 1972).

Part III. Schools

Organization & Control

What does the State Board of Education do?

THE STATE BOARD OF EDUCATION primarily concerns itself with educational standards. The members meet every other month in varying locations throughout the state to:
- develop the rules and regulations for teacher certification;
- approve teacher preparation training programs;
- determine minimum high-school graduation requirements;
- monitor basic education programs in all schools; and,
- create school accreditation standards for private schools.

Of the 18 members of the board, 2 each come from Washington's congressional districts, 1 is there to represent private schools, and the Superintendent of Public Instruction presides as Chief Executive Officer of the board. Local school board members elect their representatives on the state board.

What does the State Superintendent do?

THE SUPERINTENDENT OF PUBLIC INSTRUCTION (SPI) is a non-partisan, elected position with the duty "to supervise all matters pertaining to public schools and . . . perform such specific duties as may be prescribed by law."[1] The Office of

the Superintendent of Public Instruction (OSPI) is the organization that assists the superintendent to:
- implement state and federal laws throughout the state;
- distribute funding, in the proper proportion, to the school districts;
- help school districts with financial matters and set curriculum guidelines; and,
- produce reports for the federal government, the state legislature, and other state agencies.

The 280 employees in the superintendent's office have a more general mandate to provide educational leadership. That means taking the lead in using new technology, promoting innovation and cooperation in all levels of education, and *increasing parental involvement* throughout the school system.

What are Educational Service Districts?

WASHINGTON'S NINE EDUCATIONAL SERVICE DISTRICTS (ESD) are regional administrative offices that allow encompassed school districts to share resources and set-up cooperative teaching efforts. Individual school districts often do not have their own special education staff, computer specialists, or complete book and film libraries. The reasoning is that ESDs gives all schools access to a larger pool of resources in these areas. In 1991, Educational Service Districts employ 210 certified staff (teachers and administrators) and 670 classified staff employees.

What are the powers of a school district?

WASHINGTON'S 296 SCHOOL DISTRICTS have broad powers for making school policy: "A school district shall constitute a body corporate and shall possess all the usual powers of a public corporation, and in that name and style may sue and be sued and transact all business necessary for maintaining schools and protecting the rights of the district, and enter into such obligations as are authorized therefore by law."[2]

What do school boards do?

SCHOOL DISTRICTS MAY MAKE NEW RULES and regulations that are consistent with the broader rules of the State Board of Education and the Office of the Superintendent of Public Instruction.   Listed are several of a school board's most important duties:

- employ a local superintendent for up to a 3-year term;
- hire and dismiss all personnel from teachers and principals to school bus drivers and nurses. These employees work for the school district, not the state;
- set up courses of study consistent with standards prepared by the State Board of Education;
- determine the length of the district's school year if it is to be longer than 180 days;
- decide what grades will be grouped together in which school buildings;
- set up salary schedules for all employees, including teachers; and,
- implement the Washington Basic Education Act of 1977 and decide what waivers from that law will be requested from the State Board of Education.

What was the Basic Education Act?

IN 1977, THE STATE LEGISLATURE PASSED major educational

reforms known as the Basic Educational Act. There are two major elements to this reform that continue to impact how the Washington school system works.

On a financial level, the state formalized its constitutional obligation to fully and equally fund the state's common schools. State funds would be allocated to districts on the basis of student count. Staffing levels would also be based on student count. In a further effort to equalize funding, the state "capped" the amount wealthier districts could raise in local levies and established "equalization" formulas to give more funding to poorer districts.

The Basic Education Act also set down the ground rules for how students would receive a "basic education." Specific requirements for how long students are in school, how many hours they spend on essential subjects, and how many hours a teacher must spend in the classroom, were created for state-wide consistency.

School boards have a legal obligation to fulfill the Basic Education Act requirements. New courses may be added or subtracted from the state guidelines but overall no more than 5% difference from the state schedule is permissible.

Who serves on the school board?

THE POSITION OF SCHOOL BOARD DIRECTOR is an elected, not an appointed position. Directors serve 4-year staggered terms. Some school districts elect 5 members at large while others create 5 smaller "director districts." Candidates for school board must live within their residential school district if the position is an at-large one or reside in the director district they want to represent if the district is sub-divided.

Are school board meetings open to the public?

YES. ALL THE REGULAR MONTHLY MEETINGS of a school board are open to the public as are special meetings held between times. School boards are not required by the state to post an advance agenda; there is no requirement of timely advance public notice for regularly scheduled board meetings; and there is no guaranteed right for the public to speak at the meetings. Of course, individual districts create their own by-laws to do these things and most do so.

What is an "executive session"?

SCHOOL BOARDS MAY MEET PRIVATELY to discuss issues where the sensitivity of the matter outweighs the public's right to know. Executive sessions may be held at regular and special school board meetings after the directors announce the justification for such a meeting.

What may be decided in closed meetings?

NO FINAL VOTE MAY BE TAKEN or policy adopted in an executive (or closed) session; if such a thing occurs, the action is void and has no meaning. Votes must happen at the public meetings. The only proper use of closed sessions are these:
- Acquisition, lease, or sale of school property;
- Performance of publicly bid contracts;
- Contract negotiations;
- Personnel matters;
- Candidate qualifications for appointment to the board; and,
- Litigation and other legal matters.[3]

Are school board records open to the public?

YES, THEY ARE. "The board of directors shall maintain an office where all records, vouchers and other important papers belonging to the board may be preserved. Such records, vouchers, and other important papers at all reasonable times shall be available for public inspection."[4]

What do school directors say about their jobs?

IN SOME WAYS, SCHOOL DIRECTORS HAVE QUITE A LOT OF POWER to shape the educational policies of their district. But anecdotal evidence suggests that school board members don't feel so "in control." For one thing, they are not full-time education professionals and so they often rely heavily on school administrators' expertise to guide them through the path of complicated budget processes and programming requirements.

Then there is the money. School boards have little leeway in how to spend the pre-allocated state and federal funds they receive. Except for state "block grants" that may be spent on a wide range of things, or locally-raised funds, it is most often the case that "whoever pays the piper, calls the tune" and the state is definitely the "piper."

What does the local superintendent do?

SCHOOL BOARDS HIRE SUPERINTENDENTS to implement district policies on a daily basis. One of those daily tasks is to keep detailed financial records of the school district's receipts and expenditures. While the superintendent is primarily accountable to the local school board, he or she also has obligations to insure the school district complies with state laws and reporting requirements. Local superintendents serve up to three year terms at the pleasure of the school board.[5]

What do principals do?

PRINCIPALS MANAGE INDIVIDUAL SCHOOL BUILDINGS. They are responsible for carrying out and enforcing state and district policies level as well as the unique policies of their particular school. Principals, who must themselves hold teaching certificates, hire, fire, and promote the building's teachers and staff. Principals are also ultimately responsible for student discipline and safety at their school.[6]

Safety

May schools require the use of "release forms"?

No. THERE IS NO REQUIREMENT that students or their parents sign "release" or "consent forms" that deny them all future claims of negligence against a school district. These forms have often been the condition for student participation in interscholastic sports or clubs.

In 1988, several parents from the Odessa school district (Lincoln County) went to court when a standardized release form was a condition for their children playing school sports. The Washington Supreme Court declared the school district's release form invalid. The majority wrote that this was a situation "where public policy reasons for preserving an obligation of care owed by one person to another outweighs our traditional regard for the freedom to contract."[7] Recognizing that sports are an especially important part of school life, the court stated that "a school district owes a duty to its students to employ ordinary care and to anticipate foreseen dangers" and that such "assumption of risk" forms are invalid.[8]

Are schools always responsible for students?

No. THERE ARE LIMITS TO A SCHOOL'S LIABILITY. In June of 1979 the Grandview High School (Yakima County) Senior class held a meeting where they planned an off-campus party. When their faculty adviser learned that beer was to be served at the event, she admonished the students and reported it to the principal. The students had their party and drank their beer; upon returning, one girl was killed in a car-truck accident. She was found to have a .13% blood alcohol level. In the lawsuit that followed, the school district was *not* found negligent. The Court found that the student party was not a normal school activity; it was neither planned nor supervised by school officials, and it had their explicit disapproval, not approval. Mere knowledge (in this case, by the adviser and Vice-Principal) about the event did not create a condition of negligence.

How do schools protect students from strangers?

PARENTS SHOULD OBTAIN THE PROCEDURES that schools use to protect children from unwanted people on school grounds. Every district has to ensure that "no child will be removed from any school grounds or building thereon during school hours except by a person so authorized by a parent or legal guardian having legal custody." These rules generally only apply to students below the 9th grade.[9]

What are schools doing about the drug problem?

THE STATE'S SUBSTANCE-ABUSE PROGRAM has three main goals:
- to help students make informed decisions about drugs, alcohol, and tobacco (the use of all tobacco products, including chewing tobacco, is banned on school property);[10]
- to build a drug-free education environment; and,
- to aid schools in a drug policy with 3 parts. First, *pevention* of a drug problem, second, *intervention* in a drug problem, and third, *aftercare* for recovering students.

Parents are encouraged to get involved in drug prevention programs. One way to do this is to volunteer to serve on a school district substance abuse advisory committee.[11]

Are drug prevention programs working?

THEY SEEM TO BE. Drug use among Washington students has declined since 1988. While it is impossible to say exactly how much drug prevention courses contributed to this result, surveyed students who said they learned a lot from such courses were also much less likely to be moderate or heavy users. Drinking alcohol regularly at least once a month or occasional "binge" drinking was considered "moderate" for the test. "Heavy" consumption is the daily use of alcohol or any other sort of drug.

Results were best in the lower levels. In 1988, 17% of 6th

graders had tried drugs and 57% had tried alcohol. In 1990, the figures had dropped to 10% and 33%. The percentage of graduating seniors that had used the following drugs was as follows: tobacco (52%), alcohol (83%), marijuana (34%), and cocaine (8%).[12]

Can school officials search for drugs?

YES, AND NOT ONLY FOR ILLEGAL DRUGS. The principal or her designee may also search for weapons and stolen property.

In February of 1987, a student at Thomas Jefferson High School (King County) told the Vice-Principal that drugs were being sold in the school parking lot. The Vice-Principal had the suspected student brought in and told to empty his pockets; $230 in cash and a list of telephone-pager numbers were found. School security personnel searched the student's locker, found nothing, and then opened the student's car trunk. Finding 80.3 grams of marijuana, school officials called the police and the student was arrested. The Washington Supreme Court ruled that the warrantless search was legal: "The school officials' initial search was justified because they had reasonable grounds for suspecting that the student's car would turn up evidence that he had violated the law."[13]

What are schools doing about gangs?

SINCE 1987, CALIFORNIA-BASED GANGS have migrated to the Northwest in search of fresh drug markets. Ever since, gang-related crime has gone up steeply each year. While the state has begun some gang risk intervention programs, some cities have their own programs. They usually are community efforts since gangs and gang violence is much more than a school problem.

The Yakima school district works with the police and parks departments to offer alternative activities to youth in the most troubled neighborhoods. King County has its Regional Educational Alliance on Gang Activities (REAGA) program that offers a 2-day training course to educators on recognizing gangs and intervention techniques. The Drug Awareness and Resistance Education program (DARE) has also been expanded to teach 5th and 6th graders about avoiding gangs.

What are schools teaching about AIDS?

WASHINGTON REQUIRES AIDS (acquired immunodeficiency syndrome) education each year beginning no later than the 5th grade. Although each school district may set its agenda, AIDS education is limited to the life-threatening danger of the disease and its spread and prevention. The locally adopted program must be submitted to the Department of Health to be approved for medical accuracy.

At least 30 days before the start of the AIDS class, the school district must conduct at least one presentation to outline the AIDS curriculum and show the class materials. "No student may be required to participate in AIDS prevention education if the student's parent, having attended one of the presentations, objects in writing."[14]

Is sex education mandatory?

NO. THE DECISION TO TEACH SEX EDUCATION and how it is taught is up to each school board. Parents have a couple of rights concerning sex education. For one, "school districts shall involve parents and school district community groups in the planning, development, evaluation, and revision of any instruction in sex education and human sexuality offered as part of the school programs."[15]   Also, parents who object to the course may excuse their child from the sex education class.

May school officials give students medicine?

YES, BUT UNDER SEVERAL RESTRICTIONS. Districts must have a policy to determine who may administer medicine. They must also have a parent's current, written request and instructions concerning the medicine.   And finally, they must have an unexpired, written request and instructions from the child's doctor or dentist. If these conditions are met, then those school employees administering medicine will not be liable for any criminal actions or for any civil damages.[16]

What kind of medicine may be administered?

STATE LAW PERMITS SCHOOLS TO ADMINISTER only "oral" medicines which mean only medicines taken through the mouth.   Both pills and inhaled medicines come under that description.

Over-the-counter drugs such as aspirin, tylenol, and vitamins are considered medicine like any other and so the school needs both a parent's and doctor's request to administer these types of non-prescription drugs. Otherwise, the school is not fully protected from negligence lawsuits.

Some pills, like vitamins, may sometimes be taken as a nutritional supplement and at other times as a medicine to cure a particular illness. Since schools don't have the expertise to determine why a certain pill is taken, they require a doctors request in *all* situations.

Transportation

Who decides school bus routes?

School boards determine the transportation policies of the district. They plan the chosen bus routes and which students are to be transported.

School boards are also responsible for students having a safe path to school. Safe walking conditions means no "social hazards" as well as safe roads. Students should not be expected to pick their way through areas with drug dealing, violence, prostitution, or environmental problems like toxic waste dumps.[17]

Who is qualified to drive a school bus?

School districts can only hire certified bus drivers who have taken a training course on driving a bus and have at least one year prior experience in driving a truck or commercial vehicle. Continuing employees must take a "refresher training course" every 4 years and a basic first aid course every 4 years.

Bus drivers must also pass a complete physical exam every 4 years if they are age 18-36, every 2 years if age 37-59, and every year if over age 59.

School districts may fire a driver for a poor driving record:

"Continuing certificates will be granted to drivers with the understanding that any unsafe driving practices, violation of motor vehicle laws, or involvement in an accident which the bus driver could have prevented or an accident in which the bus driver is held to be partially or fully at fault could result in the cancellation of the school bus driver certificate. This applies to any motor vehicles the bus driver may be operating."[18]

Do districts transport non-residential students?

No, ALTHOUGH SCHOOL DISTRICTS MAY BE PERSUADED to bus non-residential students if the pick-up could be made cheaply and promptly. It is the obligation of the parents to take their child to the nearest school bus stop within the non-residential school district.

May a parent ride the school bus?

YES. THE PARENT WOULD FIRST REQUEST PERMISSION from their child's school. School officials in turn would ask the school board. If there is seating room on the bus and the board thinks the request reasonable, they will grant the parent's request.[19]

May school buses be used for other purposes?

YES. "ANY SCHOOL DISTRICT MAY CONTRACT to furnish the use of school buses of that district to other users who are engaged in conducting an educational or recreational program supported wholly or in part by tax funds or programs for elderly persons at times when those buses are not needed by that district."[20]

School districts may lease their buses to non-profit organizations to transport handicapped children or the elderly to special events but only if public commercial transportation is not reasonably available.

Who else is responsible for student safety?

THE SAFETY OF STUDENTS ON THEIR WAY TO SCHOOL is not just the responsibility of the district and its bus drivers. It is also a legal responsibility of building developers and planning commissions. Local government "shall determine if appropriate provisions are made for . . . schools and school grounds and all other relevant facts, including sidewalks and other planning features that assure safe walking conditions for students who walk to and from school."[21]

Curriculum

What are minimum graduation requirements?

THE MINIMUM SUBJECT AREAS AND CREDITS to graduate in Washington are as follows.[22] One credit is equal to one year of study in the subject.

Subject	Credit
English	3
Mathematics	2
Science	2 1/2
United States History and Government	(1)

Subject	Credit
Washington State History and Government	+ (1/2)
Contemporary World History, Geography and Problems	+ (1)
Social Studies	= 2 1/2
Occupational Education	1
Physical Education	2
Elective in above or the Arts	1
Other Elective options	5 1/2

How are textbooks chosen?

SCHOOL DISTRICTS MUST HAVE A WRITTEN POLICY explaining how and why classroom textbooks are chosen. Although parents may serve on a school district's textbook committee, alongside school staff, they must make up less than half of the total committee membership. Not all textbooks on a teacher's reading list have to be for long-term use. Textbooks can be used for a short while, experimented with, and then either accepted or rejected.

In evaluating textbooks, the "instructional material committee" may consult outside experts on the usefulness of a certain book or consult with other school districts to learn how they go about their selection process.[23]

May parents reject certain textbooks?

RARELY. PARENTS OR STUDENTS would have to make a strong case that the book has no educational merit or that the book is taught to advance religion or to be hostile towards it.

At Mead High School (Spokane County) a student and her mother objected to the use of *The Learning Tree* (by Gordon Parks) as required reading for a class. They contended that the assignment violated her First Amendment right by demeaning their religion, fundamentalist Christianity, and advancing the religion of "secular humanism." The school district's evaluation committee maintained that the book was "an appropriate element of the sophomore English curriculum."

The court sided with the school district, stating "If we are to eliminate everything that is objectionable to any of the religious bodies existing in the United States or inconsistent with any of their doctrines, we will leave public education in shreds."[24] In this situation, the court saw no advancement of religion but instead students reading "a novel with autobiographic overtones . . . for the purpose of exposing students to the expectations and orientations of Black America." There was both a secular purpose and secular effect to studying the work. Besides, the student had been given the option of leaving the class during discussions or studying another work and so there was no coercion.

On the charge that the school promoted "secular humanism," the court noted that in the language of the law, "secular" means non-religious and "humanism" was not necessarily incompatible with religion, so the association of "secular humanism" as an anti-religious doctrine in itself was invalid.

When are students tested?

WASHINGTON STATE LAW REQUIRES that all students take standardized tests in the 4th, 8th, and 11th grades. The tests cover five basic areas: Reading, English Language,

Mathematics, Science, and Social Studies. The new series of tests, which start in 1991, differ somewhat from past measurements.[25] Math problems stress overall problem solving more than computation. The reading part now tests a student's grasp of real-world writing, not artificial texts composed just for the exam.

Who uses the test results?

TEACHERS USE A PUPIL'S TEST RESULTS TO EVALUATE their progress and to determine where extra help is necessary. There is no "passing score" on the standardized tests and they are not used to determine a student's grade or to determine promotion to the next grade.

Schools use the results to see how well subjects are taught and where the curriculum needs special attention. The state uses the test to compare Washington students against the national averages or norm and to find remedial students who need the state's Learning Assistance Program.

New Subjects

Are there courses on the environment?

YES. THE PUBLIC SCHOOL CURRICULUM has begun to reflect that the majority of Washington citizens consider themselves environmentalists. In 1988, the legislature changed the common school curriculum to stress that "science be taught with special reference to the environment."[26] Three main themes

now run throughout the state's K-12 environmental education program:
- the program recognizes two systems, "natural" and "human," and the interaction between the two;
- students look at the environment from the point of view of the sciences, economics, and the humanities; and,
- environmental studies focus on solving environmental problems.

What is an "environmentally literate" student?

ENVIRONMENTAL EDUCATION GUIDELINES suggest a series of objectives in which a local or state environmental concern illustrates a teaching objective. A few examples out of many:
- students may study the relationship of the spotted owl to old growth or the damage done by driving on the ocean shore to recognize that technological growth exceeds our understanding of its impact on the environment.
- a class may investigate Indian fishing rights and the problems of waste disposal sites for lessons in environmental laws.
- working on a salmon stream or studying an environmental group are ways of actively taking part in environmental concerns.
- students may track their own use of energy, water, and solid waste to learn the impact of their personal decisions on the environment.
- a class may follow the course of some state environmental legislation to learn the importance of the political and legal process in solving environmental problems.[27]

What are schools doing with computers?

SCHOOLS EMPHASIZE THE USE OF THE COMPUTER as a tool to be used throughout all school activities and all courses. The reasoning is simple: all students will be future computer users but few students will be computer professionals. Programming and other specialized skill are are not so important as understanding computer basics such as using a keyboard and mouse, word processing, and databases.[28] The computer is a means to complete a task, not an end in itself.

What has been the effect of computers in class?

COMPUTERS DRAW STUDENTS AND TEACHERS into more group learning than might be thought. Because there is the general lack of teacher experience with computers, there is no sure path to know when and how a computer fits in the classroom. The result is that teachers need assistance from other teachers and students from other students. Cooperation is often the way to understand and use the new technology.

Is school technology up-to-date?

NO, BUT SCHOOLS RECOGNIZE THIS and are now buying more advanced and flexible technology. In the early 1980s, the Apple Computer Corporation deeply discounted the personal computers they sold to schools. The company also provided plenty of educational software to support their hardware sales. Apple thought that lots of their computers in the classroom would encourage "brand loyal" students to be Apple users as adults. However, computer technology moves quickly and the original Apple computers are now curiosity items. The result is that while schools have a lot of computers (1 for every 12 students), they also have dated computers: 64% Apple II, 17% Microsoft-Disk Operating System (MS-DOS), 12% Apple Macintosh, and 7% other machines. Interestingly enough, the business world has roughly the opposite ratio (5 MS-DOS computers to 1 Apple computer).[29]

What is "international education"?

INTERNATIONAL EDUCATION MEANS THE STUDY OF OTHER CULTURES and the global issues which link us together. An increasing number of the state's jobs, more than a fourth, are tied to international trade. Washington State trades with over 130 of the worlds 165 nations, with those countries on the Pacific Rim leading the way. The state's emphasis on international education throughout the curriculum is based on these facts.[30]

International education is also based on the idea that all nations and their respective citizens are, so to speak, "in the same boat." It is important for students to see that as diverse as the world's cultures are, they are also dependent on each other. State curriculum guidelines list several goals of international education:
- increase student exchanges with foreign schools;
- have students learn a foreign language at the earliest age possible;
- give all courses an international focus; and,
- set up speaker bureaus that enlighten students about international careers.

What's an example of international education?

THE SUPERINTENDENT OF PUBLIC INSTRUCTION provides national "idea books" that provides classroom exercises for all levels. For example, Japan is studied throughout various classes and grades. Japan's poetry may be studied through Haiku, one of its religions through Zen Buddhism, Japanese art through Relief Block prints, and Japanese methods of education by comparing them to our own. As Japan is Washington State's number one trading partner, Japan's economy and laws should come under special attention in high school.

What is "multiculturalism"?

THE BEST EXPLANATION OF MULTICULTURALISM is the belief that all cultures have equal value, that a nation's "culture isn't a rational invention; that there are thousands of other cultures and they all work pretty well; that all cultures function on faith rather than truth; that there are lots of alternatives to our own society."[31]

Are both teaching the same thing?

IN PART, YES. BOTH STRESS that international cooperation and understanding is necessary in resolving world issues. "International education and multicultural education share many of the same concerns and objectives . . . Multicultural education has had the opportunity to evolve its own pedagogy and materials which can be used in international education. Therefore, teachers may find multicultural materials and teaching techniques useful in the international education effort."[32]

Multiculturalism is a controversial topic at colleges and universities and perhaps is due to become one in the secondary schools. Advocates of multiculturalism argue that it is only fair that ethnic groups give equal attention to their own history and own heroes. They feel that the accomplishments of white European and American men have been overemphasized at the expense of studying other cultures.

Opponents argue that the assumptions of multiculturalism are simply untrue. Not all cultures and values are equal. Students should be taught to discriminate about what is true and not true, what is good and what is bad. To say that "all values are relative" does not give human reason the special place it deserves in education. Furthermore, our common ground as Americans should be stressed rather than our racial and ethnic differences.

How can parents get involved in these subjects?

THESE NEW COURSES CAN USE the professional knowledge and experience that parents can provide. Those with experience of international business and government are welcome to share this knowledge with the schools. Those parents with travel and foreign language knowledge are also valuable to these programs.

Patriotism

What do schools teach about patriotism?

"IT SHALL BE THE DUTY OF ALL TEACHERS to endeavor to

impress upon the minds of their pupils the principles of morality, truth, justice, temperance, humanity and patriotism; to teach them to avoid idleness, profanity, and falsehood; to instruct them in the principles of free government, and to train them up in the true comprehension of the rights, duty, and dignity of American citizenship."[33]

Schools are to display the United States flag during school hours. The pledge of allegiance is to be recited at the start of school assemblies and at the beginning of the day in all classrooms (although most secondary schools do this once a week). Pupils who choose not to recite the pledge must then "maintain a respectful silence."[34]

Graduating seniors must also have studied at least a year of United States history and a semester of Washington state history.

Religion

What does the law say about religious matters?

THE WASHINGTON STATE CONSTITUTION says, "All schools maintained or supported wholly or in part by public funds shall be forever free from sectarian control or influence."[35] Public schools must be neutral toward religion; that is, either encouragement or hostility towards any religion is unacceptable. Classes in religion must stress the literary and historical rather than the religious aspects of any religious materials used in the classroom.

This neutrality also applies on a personal level; a teacher may not inquire into the religious beliefs of a student nor may the student ask the same of a teacher.[36]

May prayers be said at school?

NO. PRAYERS OR THE READING OF THE BIBLE violates the separation of church and state clause of the First Amendment. Excusing students from participating in voluntary prayers or having nondenominational prayers does not change the situation. Prayers are taking place under a state agency, in this case a public school, and that is not permitted.[37]

Is a "minute of silence" acceptable?

SOMETIMES. IT DEPENDS ON ITS PURPOSE. If the policy is encouraging to religion, or if the practiced policy of "the minute of silence" entangles school functions and religion, then it will fail if challenged in the courts. Washington has no "minute of silence" in the public schools. If it did, the intent of the law would have to make the moment of silence one for "personal thoughts," not prayer.

May students form religious clubs?

YES. THE SUPREME COURT HAS RULED that public schools must give "equal access" to students' clubs, including those that meet on a basis of common political, *religious*, or philosophical interests. These groups may meet in school facilities outside of regular school hours.

Students at Westside High School (Nebraska) wanted to form a Christian club that would be open to all students who wanted to read the Bible, discuss it, and pray together. School officials refused to permit the club on the grounds that it violated the Establishment Clause of the Federal Constitution. The United States Supreme Court disagreed, maintaining that there was a "crucial difference between *government* speech endorsing religion, which the Establishment Clause forbids, and *private* speech endorsing religion which the Free Speech and Free Exercise Clauses protect. We think that secondary students are mature enough and are likely to understand that a school does not endorse or support student speech that it merely permits on a nondiscriminatory basis."[38] The Westside Christian club did not entangle church and state because it did not involve teachers, and the school clearly did not endorse the club's views.

There are limits to "equal access"; the law simply says that if a variety of student clubs exist, and they are not "directly related" to the school's curriculum, then the school must also allow religious clubs. However, schools must maintain a policy of tolerance, not endorsement, towards these clubs. Schools "cannot structure an environment in which students holding mainstream views may be able to coerce adherents of minority religions to attend club meetings or adhere to club beliefs. The State cannot disdain its responsibility for these resulting pressures."[39]

Finance

Who is financially responsible for the schools?

THE EDUCATION OF ALL WASHINGTON CHILDREN is the responsibility of the state government. The state Constitution says: "It is the paramount duty of the state to make ample provisions for the education of all children residing within its borders, without distinction or preference on account of race, color, caste, or sex" and "The legislature shall provide for a general and uniform system of public schools."[40] This being so, the state, not the school districts, is *primarily* responsible for the funding of public schools.

Where do schools get their money?

SCHOOLS RECEIVE THEIR FUNDING from three major sources. Averages of all the state's school districts show about 79% of their funding comes from the state government; 15% is raised through local school district property taxes, and 6% comes from the federal government.[41]

Where does the state government get its money?

WASHINGTON STATE RELIES PRIMARILY ON THREE REVENUE sources: the sales tax (57%), the Business and Occupation tax (17%), and state property tax (11%).[42]

Does the state lottery support public schools?

A LITTLE. LOTTERY REVENUE GOES TO ALL STATE PROGRAMS, not just education. Washington's lottery games (Lotto, Quinto, The Daily Game, and Scratch Tickets) pass on about 38% of earnings to the state's General Fund. That percentage means the lottery earns about 100 million dollars per year for the state's General Fund, an amount that makes up roughly 1.2% of total state revenue.[43]

Do timber sales support public schools?

YES, ALTHOUGH LESS SO IN RECENT TIMES. The schools receive timber money from three places: the state excise tax, the state trust lands, and the national forests.

How does the timber tax support public schools?

THE STATE COLLECTS A TIMBER EXCISE TAX that accounts for 0.3% of the General Fund. Whenever timber from *public* lands is sold, the purchaser pays a 5% tax which goes to the General Fund. Whenever timber from *private* lands is sold, the purchaser pays a 1% tax to the General Fund and a 4% tax which goes to the schools within that county.[44] Timber taxes are paid at harvest time in lieu of a property tax on standing timber.

What is the Common School Construction Fund?

WHEN WASHINGTON STATE JOINED THE UNION, the "Enabling Act of 1889" designated two sections out of each township for the support of public schools. This 1.3 million acres of trust land is managed by the state's Department of Natural Resources (DNR). The revenue from this land is used for the Common School Construction Fund and is dedicated to building schools throughout the state.

How does this trust land help the schools?

WHEN TIMBER IS HARVESTED FROM THESE LANDS, the Superintendent of Public Instruction receives 75% of the proceeds with the other 25% going to the Department of Natural Resources for management of these forests.[45]

The Common School Construction Fund is seeing hard times. Lots of the trust land is on the Olympic Peninsula where it has been set aside for protection of the Spotted Owl. And the 25% cap on log exports has kept prices down on the remaining timber. Still, 60-100 million dollars a year comes into the Common School Construction Fund.

How do the national forests support schools?

WHEN TIMBER FROM A NATIONAL FOREST IS SOLD, the National Forest Service pays 25% of the gross revenue to the county where the timber was cut. The county must distribute 50% of that amount to the public schools and the other 50% to either public roads or public schools. Timber rich counties thus receive more than timber poor counties. However, timber-rich counties have far fewer personal properties to tax for "local" money. The money from this Federal Forest Revolving Fund is distributed in proportion to the number of students in each of the counties' school districts.[46]

Do all school districts receive equal funding?

JUST ABOUT. THE BASIC EDUCATION ACT OF 1977 established the current "formula" for apportionment of funds to school districts. State financial support for "equalizing educational opportunities" means that state funds for basic education are distributed according to the number of students in a school district.[47] Other school district services are based on student count including programs for the handicapped, special education students, and bilingual students.

However, not all revenue apportionment is based on student count. For example, districts with more experienced and educated administrators and teachers will receive more funds for salaries. There is also a small school factor that gives districts with less than 300 students extra money; those districts receive as much as $10,000 per pupil as compared to the average of $3700 per pupil in state money.

How do schools get "local" money?

INDIVIDUAL SCHOOL DISTRICTS MAY SUPPLEMENT their state and federal funding by requesting a voter-approved increase in property taxes for a one to two year period.[48] These taxes are for the general day-to-day school activities and are called "Maintenance and Operations" levies. School districts may also request additional and separate property tax increases to help pay for bonds sold to build new school buildings or buy school buses.

Is there a limit to local school taxes?

YES. EACH DISTRICT HAS A DIFFERENT LIMIT to the amount of property tax dollars it can request from the voters. There are two major figures that figure into that amount, the "levy base" and the "levy lid." The "levy base" is the amount the district receives from the state (including the Basic Education allotment and all funding for special programs) plus the monies received from the federal government. The "levy lid" is set at 20% of that amount. About a third of Washington's school districts have in the past relied heavily on local taxes. These districts are "grandfathered in" to allow a "levy lid" over the 20% limit.

Who pays for new school buildings?

BOTH THE STATE AND THE LOCAL SCHOOL DISTRICT contribute for new buildings. School districts may request additional and separate property tax increases to help pay for bonds sold to build new school buildings. If the new building is for administration or athletics then the district must absorb the whole cost. But if the new building is for classrooms, then the state will contribute an average of 50% of the building's cost, depending on the relative wealth of the school district.[49] The state pays its part out of the Common School Construction Fund if there are enough timber dollars to go around. If not, districts join a waiting list to get their share of state funding.

New Directions

Where are Washington's school going?

"IN TWO DIRECTIONS" IS THE SHORT ANSWER. Changes at both the local and national levels now have the momentum. In some ways, the two trends complement each other. National educational standards and national testing call for some uniformity of results among schools. Increasing local control means letting individual schools determine their own way to obtain acceptable results.

What is the state doing to reform education?

THIS STATE'S MOST AMBITIOUS EFFORT AT SCHOOL REFORM is the "Schools For the 21st Century Program." The program's purpose is to give local school districts and individual schools the opportunity to *transform*, not *reform* public education. "Reform" often means minor changes around the edges of the educational system. And it often means "more," as in more school days in the year, more hours in the school days, and more hours on certain key subjects. The idea of the 21st Century program is to transform a school with a complete overhaul. To do this, the State Board of Education has released participating schools from many of its rules and regulations. For example, a 21st Century school may plan on scheduling a teacher's time differently to allow for more flexibility; to do so, certain collective bargaining rules would have to be waived by the local district and union. The State Board of Education would have to waive certain Basic Education requirements.

Basically, 21st Century schools are laboratories; the state hopes that these schools will provide the path to better Washington schools.

How do "21st Century Schools" work?

AS THE FOLLOWING THREE EXAMPLES SHOW, each experimental school has gone its own way in the first few years of the program. The only common thread among them is parental support. Parents often took the initiative in these projects (sometimes helping to write the original grant proposals to the State Board of Education). Parents continued to show their support by participating in and evaluating their children's new schools.

Clark Elementary (King County)

CLARK PROBABLY INVOLVES PARENTS MORE THAN ANY OTHER school in the state. In fact, parents who choose Clark also choose to work a minimum of 40 hours per child per school year. Parents may do a lot with that 40 hours: they may assist on field trips, they may be trained to help as one-on-one tutors, or they may help out as a teacher's aides. It is up to the teacher how parents can best be used.

Parents like knowing what goes on in their child's classroom and teachers profit by knowing their students' families that much better. Testing scores at Clark are up: Metropolitan Achievement Scores (MAT) scores went up from 71% to 92% in 3 years.[50]

Concrete Elementary (Skagit County)

CONCRETE ELEMENTARY IS JUST BEGINNING a 5 year project in "continuous progress." This means students are grouped together by ability rather than age-group or grade. Teachers will remain with their group of students as long as 3 years. A school survey showed 80% of the school's parents want to try the new program; a traditional grade school structure will be kept for those parents who do not want the new, experimental, program.

One parental concern is the adjustment their children will have to make when they leave the grouping-by-ability program and advance for the formal grades of junior high school.[51]

Yakima School District (Yakima County)

THIS PROGRAM IS BY FAR THE BIGGEST VENTURE IN THE STATE. Since 1988, the district has so far changed half its schools over to an "outcome-based" program. This means that students do not advance by putting in so many hours in a certain class ("seat-time"). Rather, learning class material and meeting pre-determined objectives are the measure of success.

By and large, parents have been supportive of the Yakima school district's project although the initiative for the program came from inside the school district administration. A possible change to the program is adding summer classes, the argument being that too much time in the fall is spent relearning spring lessons.[52]

Do these "experimental schools" work?

IT IS TOO EARLY TO TELL. Many of the schools that turned in numeric test scores find improvement — attendance and test scores are up while disruptions and dropouts are down. Other experimental schools grade themselves differently. Cooperation, communication, and problem solving cannot be measured by standardized tests or record-keeping. These schools could say that the learning atmosphere improved as a result of their change. As these first 33 experimental schools are risk takers, it is to be expected that some will, in fact, not improve.

What is "school-based management"?

SCHOOL-BASED MANAGEMENT is when those closest to a school make the decisions about how the school will operate. Unlike 21st Century programs, there are few changes in curriculum and teaching methods. Instead, there is a shift in who makes decisions. Teachers, administrators, staff, parents, (and sometimes students), all participate in the decisions about *their* school.[53]

There are many variations among these types of schools. Some concentrate on teachers having a major say in the school's budget and staffing levels. Other schools concentrate on involving the community's social agencies and businesses. All types of participative schools involve parents.

Washington has increased state support of these community-type schools since 1985. The law encourages these schools to focus on involving all of those directly concerned with a school. It is up to the school district to determine exactly *how* parents are involved and what sort of training they should receive to be usefully involved.[54]

What do parents say about their participation?

THE REACTION OF PARENTS IS MIXED. It is new and exciting to have a say about schools but it is also stressful and time-consuming to be involved.[55] However, the overall message was not to slow down the reforms. Specific concerns from the Bellevue school district (King County) were as follows.

• There was much concern over just how much time committees take and how they tend to diffuse responsibility. One parent, frustrated over a principal's inaction, said "Their [school authorities] answer to most questions is 'I can't make anyone do anything because this is building-based management.' I think this Program Delivery Council (PDC) is a cop-out for the district Superintendent and for some principals. There is no authority anymore."

• Parents who spent so much time on committees became aware of how much time teachers also spent on school-level concerns; this was time that could be spent in the classroom with their children.

• There was concern that the stress on *all* students achieving their full potential led to "saving" one student at the expense of the others. As one school staff member said, "If some of the parents of normal kids knew how much time we spend on disrupters, they'd be pretty upset."

• Parents were confused about their responsibilities: were they equal to the teachers and staff or not? Parents thought they needed training on *how schools work* before assuming such responsibilities; without that knowledge of rules, regulations, and precedents, they were just "token" members. A parent commented: "I have been labeled as a "parent in the know" because I am an active parent. After responding to this survey [about how school-based decisions work], I find I don't know much at all."

• Many parents interested in teacher performance were frustrated. One parent said "They [parents] are disenchanted by failure to replace a teacher. I feel a real rage building. I have no positive channels to take my concerns."

Does local control make a difference?

WE DON'T KNOW. If success is measured by a greater percentage of better educated students graduating from these schools, then the numbers are not there to either support or discredit community-type schools. If success means more students staying in school or the slower students doing better, we still don't know.

What reforms are from the "other" Washington?

WITH PRIMARY FUNDING FOR PUBLIC EDUCATION up to the

states, the federal government is left to encourage certain educational policies. Several ideas from the current administration are now in play at the national Department of Education:[56]

- National tests may be used, on a voluntary basis, at the end of the 4th, 8th, and 12th grades. These tests would concentrate on "core" subjects such as English, math, science, history, and geography. Universities will be encouraged to use these tests for admission; businesses will be encouraged to use them for hiring consideration. The test results would be a consistent way of measuring how American students compare against students from other countries. For the past decade, United States students have compared poorly.

- States may be asked to collect and publish data on their schools. The results would help parents compare one school to another: Which school has the best math test scores? Which school has the best record of retaining "at risk students"? Answers to these questions will help parents choose the best school for their child.

- There may be a national program similar to Washington state's Schools for the 21st Century program. Hundreds of schools evenly distributed across the country would break traditions and re-invent themselves free of federal red tape.

Will Congress spend more on education?

THAT IS UNLIKELY. First, the fact of the federal deficit makes for slim odds on increased spending for anything. Second, spending and the control that goes with spending, is traditionally a state and local function. Third, the federal government, which includes Congress as well as the present administration, has already seen the states increase spending on public education for much of the past decade.

What does business think about public schools?

THE WASHINGTON ROUNDTABLE, a business group that represents the state's largest corporations, has two convictions concerning the state's schools. One, it is in their immediate interest to have better public schools. The other is that major reforms are necessary to achieve the quality they want.

This assessment of the current school system is from the group's 1989 study: "The system has become a production line rather than an educational process. In effect, learning is separated into classrooms and controlled by bells, distributed through types of schools (elementary, middle, junior, high), across tracks (academic, general, technical, and vocational); and through time (twelve years, nine months a year, five days a week, six to ten periods a day). Twelve years of educational participation signifies adequate learning. Competence is established by the acquisition of sufficient credits."[57]

This assessment worries Washington businesses because they do not need lots of workers trained in simple, basic skills. Instead, they need employees who can reason, learn new skills, and think of new solutions to problems that have no one answer. Washington corporations are especially concerned that schools teach students to compete in a world economy. In a state where 1 in 6 jobs is directly tied to international trade, business needs future employees able to compete globally.

What is business's education agenda?

CORPORATE WASHINGTON WOULD LIKE TO SEE the school system change in five ways:[58]

• Business supports expanding programs that help poorer "children at risk." The idea that "an ounce of prevention is worth a pound of cure" appeals to many companies. By paying up front for programs like Early Childhood Education Assistance Program and First Steps, they see reduced welfare payments, reduced expenditures for remedial instruction, less crime, and less need for higher taxes in the future to pay for these things.

• Business favors mandatory testing of students in core subject areas. They want to see more consistent results for all students so that remedial skills do not have to be taught again when students enter the job market.

• Corporations, in general, support increased teacher salaries in an effort to draw and keep good teachers. But business also wants some form of "pay for performance" instead of blanket pay increases.

• Business would like to see teachers treated more as business professionals. There should be more year-to-year teacher education and internships with Washington businesses. Grants should be available to encourage innovation among teachers.

• More localized control is a key business issue. Authority should be taken from the state level and given to local districts. Competition between schools would be completed by implementing state-wide parental/student choice programs.

What is business doing for the schools?

IN 1990, THE EDUCATION RENEWAL INSTITUTE was created to apply business knowledge and leadership to the public schools. This group is made up of equal parts business executives and professional educators. The institute provides a forum where both groups can work together on school reform and try to come to terms on obvious policy differences.

Merit pay, "school choice", and the need for a dedicated tax increase for public schools are just some of the political issues that divide business and the parts of the education establishment. The Educational Renewal Institute is implementing, on a 6-year trial basis, some of the Business Roundtable's education agenda. With a budget of $550,000, the group is now working with four school districts (Pasco, Moses Lake, Issaquah, and Bellevue) to restructure schools without spending more money in the process. For example, the Issaquah school district is using the money to experiment with a teacher's time to allow for more in-service training.

Getting Involved

How can parents judge a good school?

ONE WAY TO FIND OUT IS TO READ THE SCHOOL'S own self-evaluation. All districts have a schedule and a process that its schools must use as a guide to regular evaluation. The review will use both the State Board of Education criteria and local standards to "focus upon the quality and appropriateness of the school's educational program and the results of its operational effort."[59]

- The school review includes the participation of parents.
- The review includes identifying what the district's students are supposed to be learning and how well individual schools are teaching them. Schools may include in the review what special programs and efforts they are making towards the student's education.
- The evaluation answers broad questions such as "What

is the district doing to achieve educational excellence?", "What is the district doing to achieve educational equity?", and "Is there consensus on school matters within the community?"

• The review may also address more immediate concerns such as staffing and class size.

• The state encourages schools to have a yearly process of setting measurable goals and a schedule of how to improve and accomplish those goals.

What help is available to parents?

LOTS. IT IS REALLY A MATTER OF DECIDING what works best for you and how involved you want to be.

If you need the answer to a specific question about schools, contact your child's school and ask the principal. They can always refer you to the expert or authority if they don't know the answer.

If your concern is with a certain type of program, say special education or programs for gifted children, it is worth your time to contact one of the state organizations dedicated to just that concern. This book lists many of those organizations in the back.

If your interest in the schools is more general, a traditional organization like the Parent-Teacher Association (PTA) may be a good place to get started.

Finally, you always have the choice of starting your own group. The focus of the group may be a specific school or district. Or the focus of the group may be to help a school with a particular problem. Some groups, like chapters of the PTA, choose to affiliate themselves with a certain school and directly involve teachers and administration. Your group may choose a different route. In any case, it is always best to notify the school of your group's goals and intentions.[60]

How can you find other concerned parents?

- Ask your child's teacher for the names of other parents with children in the class.
- Contact the civic groups in your community. Organizations like the Chamber of Commerce often have education committees where you will meet like-minded people.
- Write a letter to the editor of your local paper. Ask other parents to contact you.
- Contact some of the state organizations listed in the back of this book. They can refer you to local groups or persons in your community with similar interests.
- Attend the district's school board meeting and see who else is there. Introduce yourself and your concern.
- Check with your local library for the names of other local parent groups concerned with the schools. Visit their meeting and see if it is your kind of group.

How may senior citizens help the schools?

SENIOR CITIZENS MAY TAKE THE TIME TO VOLUNTEER for Washington's "six-plus-sixty" program. The program's purpose is to take advantage of the experience of retired people by encouraging them to share their knowledge with school children. Participating school districts create their own ways to bring children and senior citizens together. Although the program is voluntary, schools compensate volunteers for training, lunch, and transportation to and from school.

What information is available from schools?

THE FEDERAL FREEDOM OF INFORMATION ACT allows parents to learn a great deal about how schools and school districts operate. Sometimes a written request may be necessary, but an explanation of why you want the information is unnecessary.

• Ask for documentation on school policies. What is the school or district policy on homework? What is the schedule for parent-teacher conferences?

• Obtain the standardized test results by school and grade. See how your school is doing compared to others.

• Check out how students did after graduation. Were the students that began work right away ready for the work-world? Does the school ever get feedback from local businesses?

• Does the school offer courses that exceed state requirements? Are those student prepared for college? How do the students perform on college entrance exams such as the Scholastic Aptitude Test (SAT)?

• Get copies of the school board's minutes and resolutions. Get on the mailing list to receive copies of the agenda and other business papers.

• Is there an overall plan to assess how the school is doing? What are the goals of the school? Is the school working on new programs? Compare the goals of the school with the realities of the budget — do they match?

• There are a variety of useful financial figures that districts have. For example: How many dollars are spent per pupil for instruction? How much is spent per pupil for administration?

- What is the student to teacher ratio at the school? What is the ratio of administrators to teachers? Does the school provide for teacher training and education?

What is the best way to work with educators?

•KEEP AN OPEN MIND. You have a concern, but you may not know the whole story of what the school is doing. The first task is simply to get more information and to let the administrator know of your interest. Remember that they are more often than not your allies in change.

- Be persistent, be direct, and be polite.
- Schools should have a clear idea of what is expected of students and parents. Parents should in turn let schools know that they favor high standards and high expectations.
- Acknowledge what the school does well.
- Write the school official about your concern. Keep a copy for your records.
- Approach the problem where it occurs. For example, teachers have little say about a school's suspension policy; it is a principal's concern. On the other hand, the teacher is the best person to address your classroom concerns. If your question or concern is not dealt with properly, you can always move up the chain of authority.
- Don't be snowed by educational jargon. The terms usually mean something far simpler than you imagine. ("collaborative text-based learning efforts" is just one way of saying "students studying together.") Do not be embarrassed to ask what others mean.
- Don't worry about being nosey. *Public schools are your business.*

NOTES

[1] Washington State Constitution, Article III, Section 22.

[2] RCW 28A.320.010.

[3] *Beyond the Open Door* (1989) by Nancy Berla and Susan Hlesciak Hall. Also RCW 28A.505.050 and RCW 28A.335.120.

[4] RCW 28A.330.070.

[5] RCW 28A.400.030.

[6] RCW 28A.400.100.

[7] Wagenblast v. Odessa School District 110 Wn.2d 845 (1988).

[8] Same case as above.

[9] RCW 28A.605.010.

[10] WAC 28A.210.310.

[11] Parents may obtain their district's assessment of the drug problem.

[12] From Northwest Regional Educational Laboratory 1990 state-wide survey.

[13] State v. Slaterry 56 Wn.App 820 (1990).

[14] RCW 28A.400.070.

[15] WAC 180-50-140.

[16] RCW 28A.210.260.

[17] RCW 46.37(5).

[18] WAC 180-20-230.

[19] RCW 28A.160.110.

[20] RCW 28A.160.010.

[21] RCW 58.17.110.

[22] WAC 180-51-060.

[23] RCW 28A.320.230.

[24] Grove v. Mead School District 753 F.2d 1528 (1985).

[25] 4th and 8th graders will use the Comprehensive Tests of Basic Skills — Fourth Edition (CTBS/4); 11th graders will use the Curriculum Frameworks Assessment System (CFAS).

[26] RCW 28A.230.020.

[27] *Environmental Education Guidelines For Washington Schools* p 15, 27, 31, 32, 39.

[28] The dominant computer languages in the schools are LOGO (grade school), BASIC (junior high) and Pascal (high school).

[29] *1990 Educational Technology and Telecommunication* state-wide survey result Office of the Superintendent for Public Instruction.

[30] Parents are urged to get the state booklet *International Education Curriculum Guidelines*.

31 Kurt Vonnegut, Jr. as quoted in the state's *International Education Curriculum Guide*, Page 1.

32 Same source as above.

33 RCW 28A.405.030.

34 RCW 28A.230.140.

35 Washington State Constitution, Article IX, Section 4.

36 RCW 28A.400.310.

37 Abington School District v. Schempp 374 U.S. 203 (1963) and Engel v. Vitale 370 U.S. 421 (1962).

38 Board of Education of Westside Community Schools v. Mergens 110 S.Ct 2356 (1990).

39 Same case as above.

40 Washington State Constitution, Article IX, Section 2.

41 Schools actually receive more from property taxes than meets the eye. Of all property tax income, about 55% goes to the public schools. Of that 55%, one-half is State property tax, one-half is special local property taxes. *Property Tax Statistics 1990* Washington Department of Revenue p. 9.

42 *Guide to the Organization and Financing of Washington Public Schools* 1990 p. 71.

43 *Where The Lottery Dollar Goes 1990,* Lottery Headquarters 814 4th Avenue, Olympia, 98504.

44 *Guide to the Organization and Financing of Washington Public Schools* 1990 p. 71.

45 Not all trust land is timber land. State owned farm lands in Eastern Washington make the state government the 3rd largest provider of winter wheat in the state.

46 RCW 28A.520. In 1990, national timber sales brought in 36 million dollars. Skamania County received 10 million dollars of that amount. King County received 2.4 million dollars.

47 Actually, a school district's full-time equivalent (FTE) enrollment determines state allocations. FTE is a measure of full-time student hours of classroom instruction. A school district's FTE averages 95% of daily student headcount because of part-time students, early graduates, and dropouts.

48 To pass, a school levy needs a turnout of 40% of the voters in the last General Election and 60% of those must vote "Yes" *or* at least 40% that vote "Yes" must be equal to 24% of the total votes cast in the preceding election.

49 The state is required to absorb at least 20% of the cost. *Washington School Finance Primer January 1990.*

[50]   Mr. Randy Fortenberry, Clark Elementary School, Issaquah.

[51]   Dr. Don Jeanroy, Concrete Elementary School, Concrete.

[52]   Ms. Rebecca E. Scholl, Yakima School District, Yakima.

[53]   Public educators may remember that "school-based management" is what "community-type schools" were in the fifties, "decentralized schools" were in the sixties, "participative schools" were in the seventies, and "school-centered decision-making Schools" were in the eighties.

[54]   RCW 28A.240.

[55]   All comments from *Renewal and School-Centered Decision Making in Bellevue* (February 1991) by Richard W. Clark, Bellevue School District.

[56]   *AMERICA 2000 An Education Strategy* United States Department of Education, Washington D.C.

[57]   *Creating Exceptional Public Schools For the Next Century*, Washington Roundtable 1989.

[58]   By Corporate Washington, I mean Boeing, Weyerhauser, SAFECO, PACCAR, and all of the state's banks.

[59]   RCW 28A.320.200.

[60]   *Parents Organizing To Improve Schools* (1985) by Happy Fernandez is the source for much of the "Getting Involved" section.

Useful Books

Common School Manual
Counsel For Administrative Law Services — Legal Office
Old Capitol Building FG-11
Olympia, WA 98504-3211
(206) 753-2298

Among Schoolchildren (1989)
(non-fiction: one year in the classroom of a 5th grade teacher.)
by Tracy Kidder
Avon Books

Washington Education Directory
compiled and produced every year by:
Barbara Krohn and Associates
825 Securities Building Seattle WA 98101
(206) 622-3538

Parents Organizing to Improve Schools (1985)
by Happy Fernandez

Parents, Schools and the Law (1987)
by David Schimmel and Louis Fischer

Who Controls the Schools? (1978)
by Carl Marburger

Your School, How Well Is it Working (1982)
by Donald Thomas

Available from:
The National Committee for Citizens in Education
10840 Little Patuxent Parkway, Suite 301
Columbia, MD 21044-3104
1-800-NETWORK

Helpful Organizations

Academic Research

Puget Sound Educational Consortium
Miller Hall Room 300   Mail Stop DQ-12
University of Washington
Seattle, WA 98195
(206) 543-7267

Northwest Regional Education Laboratory
101 S.W. Main Street   Suite 500
Portland, OR 97204-3297
1-800-547-6339

Alternative Education

Washington Alternative Learning Association (WALA)
P.O. Box 795
Port Townsend, WA 98368
(206) 385-9252

Bilingual

Washington Association for Bilingual Education
31849 Pacific Highway South Suite 133
Federal Way, WA 98003
(206) 941-2757

Gifted Children

Northwest Gifted Children Association
P.O. Box 1226
Bellevue, WA 98009
(206) 453-1007

Government

State Toll Free Number (800) 321-2808

Office of the Superintendent of Public Instruction
Old Capitol Building   Mail Stop FG-11
Olympia, WA 98504-3211
(206) 753-6738

State Board of Education
Old Capitol Building   Mail Stop FG-11
Olympia, WA 98504-3211
(206) 753-6715

Washington State School Directors Association
200 East Union Avenue
Olympia, WA 98501
(206) 753-3305

Governor's Council on Education Reform and Funding
Stephen Nielson, Director
100 Insurance Building
Olympia, WA 98504

Homeschooling Support Organizations

Washington Home Schooling Organization (WHO)
Western Division
P.O. Box 938
Maple Valley, WA 98038
(206) 432-3935

Washington Home Schooling Organization
Eastern Division
P.O. Box 157
Bickleton, WA 99322
(509) 896-2315

Family Learning Organization
P.O. Box 7256
Spokane, WA 99207-0256
(509) 467-2552

Moby Dick Academy
Box 236
Ocean Park, WA 98640
(206) 665-4577

Parent Advocacy Groups and Organizations

Washington State Parent Teachers Association (PTA)
2003 65th Avenue West
Tacoma, WA 98466-6215
(206) 565-2153

Citizen's Education Center Northwest
105 South Main Street
Seattle, WA 98104
(206) 624-9955

Private Schools

Washington Federation of Independent Schools
2300 South Washington
Tacoma, WA 98405
(206) 752-3324

Rural Schools

National Rural Development Institute
Western Washington University Miller Hall 359
Bellingham, WA 98225
(206) 676-3576

Rural Education Center
Cleveland Hall, Washington State University
Pullman, WA 99164-2136
(509) 335-8118

Special Education

Washington State Parent Educator Partnership Project (WSPEP)
12320 80th Avenue South
Seattle, WA 98178
1-800-422-GOAL

Parents Advocating Vocational Education (PAVE)
6316 South 12th
Tacoma, WA 98465
(206) 565-2266
1-800-5PARENT

Technology

Seattle Technology Alliance for Resources and Planning (START)
257 100th Avenue NE
Bellevue, WA 98004
(206) 637-9848

Teen Parents

Washington Alliance Concerned With School Age Parents
2366 Eastlake Avenue East #408
Seattle, WA 98102
(206) 323-3926

Unions

Washington Education Association (WEA)
33434 8th Avenue South
Federal Way, WA 98003
1-800-622-3393

(Classified Employees)
Public School Employees of Washington
4910 'A' Street SE
Pacific, WA 98047
(206) 852-3880

Index

ORDER FORM

_____ copies @ $5.95 $_____
+ 8.2% ($0.49) sales tax per copy $_____
+ $1.50 handling first copy ($0.75 others) $_____

                    Total Enclosed $_____

20% discount for orders over 10.

Checks/money orders payable to: Bastian Books

Name: _____

Address: _____

City: _____ State: ___ Zip _____

Mail to: Bastian Books
                                P.O. Box 541
                                Enumclaw, WA 98022

If you also wish to order our 1992/1993 edition for the same
price check box below and include your fee.

☐

Notes

Notes

Notes